She will
KNOT

A WOMAN'S GUIDE FOR LETTING GO

SASHA ENID

DEDICATION

In loving memory of my grandmother, whose words continue to be a reminder that happiness is still worth fighting for.

And I dedicate this to you, woman who is struggling to let go. If you've gotten your hands on this book, I pray that God will give you the strength to overcome whatever you are going through.

Read on, it might just be exactly what you needed.

ACKNOWLEDGMENTS

There are a group of women whom I have to thank and acknowledge because without them I wouldn't have been able to finish writing this book. In one way or another, whether great or small, each of these women did something that helped me get through this process of letting go.

Gloria Rivera (my mother), Jessica Perez, Ligia Diaz, Lissie Diaz, Elizabeth M. Rivera, Daiana Mercedes, Allie Huertas, Geneva K. Diwan, Cynthia Almazan,.

There are so many more people I could mention and some who preferred to remain anonymous but these are the ones that stood out the most. Never have I seen so many women come to the aid of another in a time of need. Maybe you don't know what you did or how you played a part in this but I will never forget it. Thank you.

Last but not least, to my dad and my brother. Thank you for being my protectors and my supporters in all of this and thank you for helping this book become a reality.

CONTENTS

Preface

As I wrote this book, I wrote it thinking of you. Although it was therapeutic for me, I wrote it especially for you. I went through a season of my life that I don't wish on anyone, and in which I had to let go of people I really cared about. Unfortunately, we all go through a season of letting go of people and even places and things we love. But my desire with this book was to allow God to help me through my season of letting go, so that I could not only share it with you, but help you through your process as well.

There are some things I want you to keep in mind as you read this book. First of all, I wrote it as a step-by-step process and although I believe all the steps I've provided must take place in order to let go, I by no means think that the steps need to be taken in the exact same order or that they are the only steps you'll have to take. This book is a record of the steps in the order they happened for me, but that doesn't necessarily mean you will go through them in the same order. Some of the steps also overlapped each other in my process, but everyone's process is unique to their situation.

There may also be other things involved in your letting go process that I don't mention here. That being said, I believe this book should be read with wisdom and with openness of mind and heart so that the Holy Spirit may also direct you in your process and in your decision making. I believe God has given me the wisdom to share these steps but He is also able to give you wisdom on the decisions and steps you must take.

I wrote this book over a span of time. I wrote it as I went through each step of the process of letting go. I began writing it in September 2017 two months after I began my letting go process. Some of the emotions are very raw and real and you will see that throughout the book. I wanted you, as the reader going through the situation, to know that I was empathizing with you as you went through it too. You can choose to read this book as you go through your process or you can read it in the pace you desire.

With that being said, if you are reading this and you are in a situation in which you're having a hard time letting go, then I urge you to continue reading and to follow the instructions and guidance within this book. Each chapter carries different steps in the process of letting go. Perhaps not every chapter is for you, but maybe it's for someone close to you. I've also found over the course of this book that many of the people I met who thought they had let go, were only really halfway through the process, and maybe that's your case.

So, however it is that you choose to take this journey, the important thing is that you take it. God has something incredible waiting for you on the other side if only you are courageous enough to let go of those things that bind you. I was once afraid, and too knotted up in my situation to let go. But here I am, a living testimony of what can happen when you choose to obey God and finally let go.

So I pray that you will read this book with wisdom and that you will be able to discern what God's good, pleasing and perfect will is for your life as you make decisions about letting go. May God direct you and guide you and may this book give you hope and support in your time of difficulty. Thank you for embarking on this journey with me.

-Sasha Enid <3

She Will Be Free

For too long she has stood on the sidelines
Watching life pass her by.
For too long she has looked to the side
Wondering why her, why not I?
For too long she has forgotten
Whom she was called to be,
And why?
Because she's holding onto something
That God never intended for her eyes.
And no she's not blind.
She knows this is not God's plan,
That it's nowhere close to divine.
But she hides, and she lies,
Pretending everything is fine,
Because my, what would they say
If they really knew that sometimes she desired to die?
No, not suicide, just some freak accident
To get her out of this bind.
Is she losing her mind?
This can't be what God had mind.
But I'm here to tell you that those who seek find.
So if you seek to be free,
Then you must unbind yourself
And unwind yourself
Until you find yourself.
Because she's still in there.
That girl with the dreams, who desired to be free.
That girl who loved life
And knew what she was meant to be.
But I warn you, when you discover her,
They're going to try to cover her.

They're going to try to snuff the light out of her,
Tell her she can't do it and that she won't do it,
But she will do it.
And she will not be afraid.
And she will not be delayed,
And she won't be refrained.
No,
Because now she knows her name,
And she knows to whom she belongs to.
Over her heart His name is engraved,
Jesus of Nazareth who could not be detained
by the grave,
Whose love for her is the strength that reminded her
that because He overcame,
She's more than a conqueror.
She's more than enough, more than sufficient.
And no one else has to tell her who or what she isn't.
See, He has risen,
So she no longer has to be imprisoned.
So no,
She will not give up
And she will not be stopped.
Because that would require her to stop moving.
And she just can't do that
Because something in her spirit is brewing.
Reminding her that after all the time she's wasted,
She has to catch up and it's her duty.
So she will not rest and she will not sleep
Until she finds the strength to see what's underneath.
For she is not what she sees,
She is not skin deep
And she is not what others have told her to be.
For I am her and she is me

And I'm every woman desiring to be free.
I am you and you are me,
And we are queens joined by a common enemy.
Lack of identity, falsehood,
All tied up in that which we could not release,
But today that will cease.
For we must take a stand, and I demand,
That we take back our destiny.
Daughters of the Father remember me,
Remember us,
Clothed in strength and dignity.
For Proverbs 31 is just
A reminder of who we're meant to be.
We no longer have to be bound to that slavery
Because we have been found by the Savior King,
Son of the Living God from eternity to eternity,
Alpha and Omega, Creator of everything,
The One who reigns forever,
And the One who sets the captives free.
So let go my sisters,
For freedom awaits.
He extends His hand towards you,
Now it's your move to make.

-Chapter One-

INTRODUCTION

"He has sent me to heal the brokenhearted, to proclaim liberty to the captives, and the opening of the prison to those who are bound;"—Isaiah 61:1

Let it go. If ever there was a more insulting thing to say to a person who is experiencing a life change or a loss, it's *just let it go.* As if letting go were the simplest thing in the world to do. It's not. Letting go is a journey, a very painful one at that; and you and I my friend, are about to embark on it. That's why this is not just another feel good book about how the grass is greener on the other side.

You see, as I write these words, I'm going through a season of change in my life. It is a season of letting go of the old and letting go of those things that had me all tied up. But as I loosen myself from those things that were holding me back, I'm realizing that as much as the grass seems greener on the other side, getting over that fence isn't going to be easy. This is hard. This is painful. This is frustrating, and I hate it. Maybe that's exactly how you're feeling right now too, or were at some point.

If that's the case, then I hope you're ready to join me, because this is going to be our journey to discovering how to let go and let God, as painful as it may be. Together we'll take a look at the life of a woman who faced the task of letting go with courage and resilience. Her name is Rebekah. Her story can be found in the book of Genesis, but I think you'll discover that her story can also be found woven right into yours. Rebekah's life has been a source of influence and motivation in my life through this season of releasing and transitioning, and I believe her story can do the same for you.

But before I get into her story I want to tell you something. If you're holding this book and you're in the midst of the process of letting go, then it is no coincidence. You've either had trouble letting go of something in your past or you are currently facing a decision of whether to let go or keep holding on. I want to encourage you, and I want to genuinely take this journey with you.

Sometimes life just happens and we get ourselves mixed up and knotted up into situations that almost seem impossible to let go of. Maybe because for so long we have felt that those things were holding onto us and had us tied down. But I want to challenge that pattern of thinking right now because God did not call you to be bound up or tied up, but He did call you to freedom (Galatians 5:1).

So if you decide to be free, because it is a decision, then I give you fair warning that the path to letting go of the things we have tied ourselves to, is not an easy one. It will be a rollercoaster of a journey. You will cry but you will also laugh. You will feel empty at times, but you will also feel full. You will be angry, and you will be happy. You will have regrets, but you'll also learn to forgive. It will be a crazy ride full of mixed emotions BUT at the end of it, you WILL be free, and yes, that freedom IS worth fighting for.

I know this because as I'm going through this journey I see the finish line. But just before the finish line there's this glass wall ahead of me and I can see the other side but breaking through that glass is one of the most painful things I've ever had to do. I may get scratched up, bruised up, bleed out, but as I see the other side, I can tell you the grass is greener.

Now as I look behind me I don't look at what I left behind, but I look at you who follow this path. As I write these words, tears swell up in my eyes as I think about how hard this must be for you because I've been there. But I'm willing to break through that glass wall and make a way for you to walk through as well. My prayer is that God will pour over you the same strength and courage that He has poured over me to get through this season of my life.

With that being said, I recite the words of Isaiah 61:1-3 as a declaration of faith over this book:

"The Spirit of the Lord God is upon me,

Because the Lord has anointed me

To preach good tidings to the poor;

He has sent me to heal the brokenhearted,

To proclaim liberty to the captives,

And the opening of the prison to those who are bound;

To proclaim the acceptable year of the Lord,

And the day of vengeance of our God;

To comfort all who mourn,

To console those who mourn in Zion,

To give them beauty for ashes,

The oil of joy for mourning,

The garment of praise for the spirit of heaviness;

That they may be called trees of righteousness,

The planting of the Lord, that He may be glorified."

Prayer

Father,

I thank You for my sister reading this book. I thank You because despite what she may be going through I know that even now You have not forsaken her. I know that even if she may feel that You are far away, You are right there with her. May Your love surround her and fill her with the courage and strength to make difficult decisions. May Your presence be with her as she reads this book and goes through her own process of letting go. Thank You because I know You hear us when we call out to You.

Amen.

-Chapter Two-

THE STORY OF REBEKAH

"…And she said, I will go." –Genesis 24:58

As I was in prayer one day, asking God to help me to let go, I felt the voice of God speak the name "Rebekah" into my spirit. I picked up my Bible and began to read her story in the book of Genesis. Almost immediately I began to draw connections between things I was going through in my letting go process, and Rebekah's life. It was then that I realized that Rebekah's life was the outline God had laid out for me as a guide for learning to let go. So I want to share her story with you before we begin embarking on this process of letting go.

Rebekah's story begins in the book of Genesis chapter twenty-four. But in fact, Rebekah's story doesn't begin with Rebekah at all, it begins with Abraham. Now many of you may know a bit of Abraham's story. He was a man of faith whom God called out of his land and asked to go to a land that He would show him.

Abraham obediently leaves his father's household and takes his wife and moves to where God shows him. In Abraham's obedience, God promises him that he will multiply his seed and that he will be a Father of many nations. Now Abraham's wife was barren and this promise was made to Abraham when he was already an old man.

However, God keeps His promise to Abraham and he

and Sarah (his wife) end up having a son whom they name Isaac. Let's fast forward a little. So Abraham is now in Canaan, the land God promised him, and God has made him extremely wealthy and given him favor. However, Abraham's wife Sarah has just passed away and Abraham is much older and knows that soon his time will come too.

So, Abraham asks the oldest servant of his house to find a wife for his son Isaac (something that was culturally acceptable and normal in those days). But Abraham's request comes with specifications. Abraham makes his servant swear an oath that he will not find Isaac a wife from Canaan (the land they were currently living in). The reason for this was that Abraham wanted his son to find a wife from his own people. He did not want Isaac to marry one of the Canaanite women because the Canaanites believed in and worshipped pagan gods.

Abraham makes his servant swear an oath that he will go back to the land where Abraham's family resides and find a wife for his son from there. The servant says to Abraham, "what if the woman I find doesn't come with me? Should I take Isaac to her?" (Genesis 24:5) Abraham tells his servant that he is under no circumstances allowed to take Isaac back to that land because Canaan is the land God promised to Abraham and his descendants and Isaac should not leave Canaan. Abraham goes on to tell his servant that God will help him have success on his journey and that if the woman does not wish to return with him, then the servant will be released from the oath.

The servant sets out on his journey with ten camels and goods back to the land of Mesopotamia in the city of Nahor (where Abraham was from), and he arrives outside the city by a well where he makes his camels kneel to rest at evening time (the time when the women come to draw water from the well). The servant prays to God and asks Him to give him success on this day. He says to God, *"I'm here at the well where the women come to draw water, let it be that when I ask a woman for a drink of water that she will give me to drink and that she will offer to give water to my camels as well, then I will know that You have shown me kindness and answered my request"* (Genesis 24:13-14).

As Abraham's servant is finishing his prayer, he sees a young woman walking down with a pitcher on her shoulder. This is none other than Rebekah, who happens to be the daughter of Bethuel, whom is the son of Nahor, whom is Abraham's brother. A little confusing, but basically Abraham is Rebekah's grandfather's brother. This means that she is from Abraham's family, which was part of Abraham's request to his servant. The Bible also lets us know that Rebekah was very beautiful and also a virgin, which speaks to her purity and character.

Rebekah goes down to the well and fills her pitcher with water. When the servant sees her, he runs up to her and asks if he can have a drink of water. Rebekah quickly lowers down her pitcher and gives him to drink. When the servant finishes drinking, Rebekah offers to give his camels water to drink as well, until they are finished drinking (meaning until the ten camels are satisfied).

Rebekah quickly empties her pitcher of water into the trough (which was a long narrow open container used for animals to drink out of) and she runs back to the well to draw more water until she had drawn enough for all ten camels to drink to satisfaction. The servant watched Rebekah in wonder as he pondered if God had just answered his prayer. When she had finished giving the camels to drink, Abraham's servant gave her a gold nose ring and two golden bracelets and asked her whose daughter she was, and if there was room in her household for them to stay the night.

Rebekah explained that she was the granddaughter of Nahor (Abraham's brother) and that there was plenty of room for the servant and his camels at their house. Upon hearing this and realizing that God had led him right to Abraham's family, the servant bowed his head and worshipped God. So Rebekah ran to her mother's house and told her all that had happened. When her brother Laban heard of what had happened he ran out to the well to meet the servant and brought him to the house.

At Rebekah's house the servant was given food, but he refused to eat until he could explain to Rebekah's family why he was there. So the servant explains the whole situation, that Abraham had sent him to find a wife for Isaac, and that God had answered his prayer in Rebekah.

When Laban (Rebekah's brother) and Bethuel (her father) heard this they both agreed that this must come from the Lord and that they could do nothing to stop it. They said, "Take Rebekah and go on your way, and let her be your master's wife as God has spoken". The servant brought jewels and clothing to Rebekah and brought precious gifts to Rebekah's brother and mother as well. Abraham's servant and the ones who were with him ate and drank through the night with

Rebekah's family.

When morning came, Abraham's servant said, "now send me on my way to my master", but Rebekah's mother and brother said to him, "Let Rebekah stay with us at least ten more days and then she may go with you". Abraham's servant insisted that they let him go since he had already found what he came for. Rebekah's mom and brother then said, "Let's ask Rebekah what she wants to do instead".

They called Rebekah in and asked her, "Will you go with this man?" Rebekah responded, "Yes I will go". Then the servant and his men, and Rebekah and her maids, went on their way and her family blessed her. They set out into the desert on a journey of about 400-600 miles back to Canaan.

Around evening time when Rebekah was finally arriving in Canaan, Isaac was in the field meditating when he saw the camels in the distance. Rebekah also looked into the distance and when she saw Isaac, she asked the servant, "who is that man coming to meet us?" The servant said, "That is my master". Rebekah covered her face with her veil as Isaac approached. The servant told Isaac all that had happened.

Then Isaac brought Rebekah into his mother's tent and he married her, and Isaac was comforted after the death of his mother, Sarah. Rebekah goes on to have twins with Isaac which she names Esau and Jacob. Jacob goes on to have twelve children of his own whom then become the twelve tribes of Israel. One of these tribes, the tribe of Judah would hold the lineage that would lead to the birth of Jesus Christ, whom we now thank for salvation.

Rebekah found herself confronted with the decision of letting go of her family and comfort to move to a strange land and marry someone she had never even met. But through courage and faith Rebekah is able to overcome the hardship of letting go and she is able to embark on the unknown which lead to her becoming part of a promise that would transcend her own lifetime and impact all of ours. But what if she hadn't let go?

Prayer

Father,

I ask that my sister be able to connect with the life of Rebekah. I pray that she may see glimpses of her own life and be able to relate to Rebekah's life as she continues to read this book. We are part of one body in You Lord, only separated by time, but all going through similar circumstances.

May we learn from Rebekah's life what it means to let go, what it means to move forward, and what it means to fulfill our part in Your great purpose.

In Jesus name, Amen.

-Chapter Three-
SHE WILL KNOT DO THE BARE MINIMUM

"Come to Me, all you who labor and are heavy laden, and I will give you rest."—Matthew 11:28

STEP 1: ACKNOWLEDGING YOUR CURRENT STATE

Work. Work. Work. Sound familiar? Maybe it's because I'm quoting the lyrics of your life. My life too if I'm being honest. Do you ever feel like your life is just a never ending to-do list where you just work and work and no one really appreciates all the effort you're putting in, and yet they have the audacity to expect or even demand effort on your part? Yet somehow, you just can't bring yourself to say no, because in some way you enjoy being able to say that you accomplished it.

But don't you just get tired sometimes? Don't you get tired of carrying all the burden of the world on your shoulders? Doesn't it get old to have to deal with everyone else's issues, while no one (not even yourself) stops to acknowledge yours? That's exactly how I was feeling before I let go. I was overburdened and overworked, and the saddest part was that it had become normal for me.

But what does work have to do with letting go? It has everything to do with it. In fact if you're anything like me (hardworking, persistent, refusing to do the bare minimum) then that is exactly why letting go might be so much harder than it seems to be for others. But before I continue, let's look back at

Rebekah's life.

When we're first introduced to Rebekah, we see that she is greeted by a stranger who asks her for a drink. Rebekah not only gives him water to drink, but she offers to water his ten camels as well. More specifically she states, *"I will draw water for your camels also, until they have finished drinking"* (Genesis 24:19 ESV). So I'm going to go ahead and assume that after a long journey these camels are thirsty.

Now, Rebekah offers to draw water for them until they're finished drinking, or until they're satisfied. Do you know how much water a camel can drink at a time? A camel can actually drink up to thirty gallons of water at a time. I'm not great at math but isn't 30 gallons x 10 camels something like 300 gallons of water? Talk about work ethic and determination. Why would Rebekah do this for a complete stranger?

I believe that Rebekah was accustomed to doing hard work. No woman in her right mind who is not used to working hard is going to volunteer to do so much for someone they've just met. But I'm going to take this a step further. Abraham's servant's request to God was, *"Let the young woman to whom I shall say, 'Please let down your jar that I may drink,' and who shall say, 'Drink, and I will water your camels'—let her be the one whom you have appointed for your servant Isaac"* (Genesis 24:14 ESV). The servant's request was that the girl who was meant for Isaac would offer to water the camels also. But Rebekah goes above and beyond. Not only does she water the camels but she waters them until they are all done drinking. She could have stopped at just offering to give them *some* water, but she didn't do the bare minimum. That is the key we're about to focus on.

Rebekah was an over-achiever and many of us women who struggle to let go are over-achievers as well. Now, when I say over-achiever your mind may automatically think of school achievement, but that's not what I'm referring to here. Many of us are over-achievers in our relationships and personal lives. We go above and beyond for the things and people we care about and we don't quit until we've achieved our goal. We are fighters. But we over-achievers have this hamartia, this tragic flaw, we are not satisfied with the bare minimum.

It goes without saying that we *hate* giving up; and letting go feels a lot like giving up. In fact, we will go above and beyond looking in every small corner of our lives for a possible solution before we give up. We will go above and beyond because we will not look like quitters, we will not appear to be failures. But I will let you in on a little secret. Although it may be your downfall when it comes to letting go, when used correctly, your inability to quit while you're ahead is the key to getting you through this.

Even though it is difficult to get the over-achiever to come to a place where they are ready to let go, once they are there, there's no turning back. There's no looking back for she who refuses to do the bare minimum, because now she will do everything in her power to move past this, because this, whatever this is, will not break her. It will not keep her down, and she will go above and beyond to prove that she can and will do what is necessary to get ahead. I applaud you over-achiever, my modern day Rebekah, because as much as you are hurting you are going to get past this.

But speaking of Rebekah, let's discuss a little about what her name means. The name Rebekah means, captivating, knotted cord (now you get the title of the book). Or in Hebrew, a tied up calf or lamb, one that is peculiarly choice or fat. So this is a strange combination of definitions for a name. The over achiever in me didn't stop there. I did some digging! When I dug deeper I found that Rebekah's name is actually making reference to something so beautiful and valuable that it is tied up.

Now remember that Rebekah's name is of Hebrew descent so its meaning has to do with the lifestyle of the time period in which riches could be calculated by possessions, usually of animals and goods. Her name refers to the choice or fat calf, it refers to the one that is most valuable, the healthiest, the one that is worth the most. It is the prized possession of the owner, an animal so valuable that it is tied up so that it will not escape.

If we look at Rebekah's story we see a little of that. If you recall, Rebekah's father, Bethuel, initially had a positive reaction. He and Rebekah's brother Laban tell Abraham's servant to take her because this could be nothing more than a divine plan of God. However, the next day, when it was time for her to go, her brother Laban and mother, didn't want to let her go. They wanted her to stay longer. They insisted that she stay another ten days.

Can I just interject something here? So in ancient Israel, when a marriage arrangement was taking place, it was usually the parents of the bride who made the arrangements for marrying her off (Robinson, M.A. 2012). My head-scratching question here is, why is

Laban postponing Rebekah's marriage by asking for her to stick around longer? And where is Rebekah's father, Bethuel in all this? Thankfully, Rebekah decides to leave right away, but what would've happened if she had listened to Laban, a voice who had no say or authority in the matter? He would have delayed her from her purpose. You must be mindful of voices that give you advice but have no authority to do so. Their advice usually gets you more tied up than you already are. Laban just wanted to keep Rebekah tied up. Perhaps it is because he knew her value.

But just like Rebekah, you are that prized possession, you are that choice calf. You are the above and beyond calf of the herd. You are valuable, and your value will draw both good and bad things. What will you allow to enter into your life? Or better yet, what have you already allowed to enter into your life? What is it that's holding you back now? What or who is it that has you all tied up? What is stopping you from moving on to fulfill your part in God's greater purpose?

Often times women of value end up wrapped up by situations and people that hold them back. When they do get caught up in these types of toxic situations or relationships, they lose sense of their own value. They are so overworked, and in a sense underpaid or undervalued, that they begin to believe that they have no value. This often leads to low self-esteem.

Low self-esteem is a product of lost identity. But when you know who you are, you begin to raise your standards of who and what you allow to influence or become a part of your life. However, when you don't know who you are, you don't know what you're worth and therefore you allow people to treat you however they want. If you don't know who you are, I invite you to study the Scriptures and read what they have to say about you.

Maybe you've read them before and thought, "Well yeah that might apply to other people but not to me". You need to begin to let Scripture become personal to you so that it can minister to your life. I tell you now, if you don't begin to accept your true value as given to you by God, you will never get past this stage of going above and beyond to resolve something that was never meant for you to begin with. The reason you will do this is because when you are a woman that goes above and beyond, you want and expect the things and people that surround you to be above and beyond, and when they aren't you make it your personal responsibility to make sure they are. That's you not

Be mindful of voices that
give you advice
but have no authority
to do so.

accepting the bare minimum again. We get so caught up in wanting to make everything around us better that sometimes we bind ourselves to things we were never meant to be bound to. We get caught up in trying to bring something up to our standards, not realizing that it is actually diminishing our value the more we hold on to it.

You need to have the wisdom to see what is worth investing your time into and what is not. If you don't discern this, then you will end up investing time in something or someone that isn't meant to go above and beyond with you; and that is precisely how we end up tied up in bad situations.

You need to be able to read the times and seasons of your life in order to discern when your time is up in a certain place, or with a habit or with a person or group of people. You need to be able to decipher the clues your life is giving you. You need to know when to let go even if it feels like you're giving up. The fact of the matter is that although we've been taught that giving up is a sign of failure, sometimes it is exactly what we need to do in order to succeed.

The Bible says in Psalm 46:10 *"Be still and know that I am God"*. That phrase "be still" in the original Hebrew actually means "to fail, to abandon, to let it go". So what is God saying? God is saying that sometimes you need to let it go and just accept that He is God. But the problem is that we don't know who God is and that's why it is so hard for us to just leave it in His hands.

Sometimes we are trying so hard to make something work and God is saying, "Stop trying! Let me do it!" So I challenge your over-achieving self to take this moment in your life to really get to know who God is, because your lack of knowing who He is, is directly linked to your inability to let go. We often don't let go because we don't trust that God is really going to see us through. When we doubt that God will come through for us, we are doubting His love for us and when we doubt His love for us, we question His very essence because He is love.

Maybe you struggle with understanding God's love because you've failed to receive it at some point in your life. But I'm willing to bet that you have loved before. Whether it be your own child or a parent or sibling etc. Let's take a child for example. If you're not a mom just imagine for a moment that you are. Let's say that someone is trying to hurt your child, this infant baby that you brought into this world through the pain of labor. Now, I'm willing to bet that you would do anything in your power to defend that baby from harm. Keeping that in mind, I want you to look at this verse from Isaiah 49:15 with me. This is God speaking. It states, *"Can a mother forget the baby at her breast and have no compassion on the child she has borne? Though she may forget, I will not forget you!"*

I want you to meditate on those words. If you as a mother would not forget to care for your own child, how much more will God have compassion and care for you? If what is holding you back from letting go is the fact that you believe you will have to fend for yourself and figure things out on your own after you let go, then I implore you to give God a chance to come through for you.

Before I came to the decision of letting go I was afraid that I wouldn't be able to make it on my own. Realistically, I wasn't supposed to be able to make it on my own. But God used different people to provide for my every need, because when you walk in obedience with God He will always back you up. If He came through for me, He will see you through as well. So be still (let it go) and know who God is in your life. There is nothing you can do that will stop Him from loving you. The Bible says that even when we are faithless, He is faithful (2 Timothy 2:13).

Some of us are so worried that we will let God down or that we will let other's down or even let ourselves down, that we keep holding onto things we were never meant to hold onto. We feel so over-burdened that we begin to question God. But the Bible teaches us that God's yoke is easy and His burden is light (Matthew 11:30). If your burden is heavy then it's probably not from God.

So, what are we burdening ourselves with? What burdens are we carrying that God never asked us to take on? In fact, what burdens are we carrying that God has already asked us to give to Him. The Bible also instructs us in Psalm 55:22 to cast our burdens on the Lord, because He will sustain us.

You might be asking yourself, how do I do that? How do I cast my burdens on the Lord? You begin by learning to let go and let God and you do that by first convincing yourself that you need to let go. As I said before, sometimes we think we are going to let people down if we let go but we forget that God still has a plan for those people.

We love people that we know we need to let go of BUT GOD loves them more. We want to help fix things BUT GOD is the solution. We think that WE have to be

...although we've been taught that giving up is a sign of failure, sometimes it is exactly what you need to do in order to succeed.

the ones to solve everyone's problems, BUT GOD can solve them with or without you. Remember that all things hold together in Christ (Colossians 1:17), so if He's the one holding everything and everyone up, then how can *you* possibly let anyone down? You're not the one holding them up to begin with. People's lives will go on with or without you. The most you can do is pray from a distance. Don't let pity for others stop you from making tough decisions. Take a page from Rebekah's life.

Although Rebekah's family wanted her to stick around, Rebekah made the quick and courageous decision to let go despite the fact that she was a hard worker and that her family probably depended on her labor. What makes me come to this conclusion is that Rebekah must have been physically strong in order to draw water for all of those camels until they were done drinking.

The Bible records that Rebekah was drawing water from a well using a pitcher and that she was running back and forth from the well to draw water for the camels. Even if she only drew one jar of water for each camel, she had to draw it from the well ten times and run to the camels to give it to them. This girl had some intense physical strength, so I can only assume that

Rebekah must have been accustomed to hard work in her household and that her family probably depended on her labor.

Another thing that impressed me about Rebekah was how quickly she was willing to leave her home and land to leave with a stranger to travel through the desert and get married. I do want to acknowledge the culture of the time and the fact that marrying was the expectation for women at that time, but there's something that strikes me as odd here. When Rebekah's mom and brother asked for Rebekah to stay an extra ten days Rebekah decided to leave right away anyway. The decision was hers to make and she chose not to stay any longer. This makes me think that the unknown future was more appealing to Rebekah than her current situation.

Maybe Rebekah was over-worked in her household. Maybe she was being taken advantage of. Maybe she was lonely and wanted to be married off already. I don't know what was going through Rebekah's mind at that time, but what I do know is that she chose to leave and she refused to wait any longer. In doing so she received her reward. I think there is something to learn from Rebekah. We need to know when we've done enough. We need to know how to let go of things in the past when a new season approaches.

So I ask you again, what's holding you back? What are the seasons in your life pointing you towards? What burdens are you holding onto that God never asked you to take on? What is it that's delaying you?

Questions for Reflection:

1. Has being overworked and overburdened become normal for you? When did that start happening?

2. What is the worst that can happen if you let go of one of the things that is burdening you?

3. How can you apply your hard work and determination to helping yourself let go of things that are holding you back?

4. When was the last time you took time to value yourself?

5. What can you do now to value yourself and/or take care of yourself better?

Notes:

Prayer

Father God,

Right now I just want to pray for my hard working sister. Although she has exhausted her strength I declare new strength in her right now.

I pray that in her hard work she learns to value herself, for she is Your prized possession. Let her see herself the way that You see her. That she may see that she is worthy of being loved, honored and respected. I pray that You give her the strength to pull away and know that she deserves to be valued.

In Jesus name, Amen.

-Chapter Four-

SHE WILL KNOT BE DELAYED

"Behold, now is the accepted time; behold, now is
the day of salvation."
—2 Corinthians 6:2

STEP 2: MAKING THE DECISION

When I was a little girl I had a jar full of pennies. I had been collecting pennies for quite some time, and at my young age, I thought I had a lot of money. One day my grandfather offered to give me a twenty dollar bill in exchange for all my pennies. Mind you I'm pretty sure I didn't have twenty dollars' worth of pennies in that jar. But when my grandfather made me that offer and I looked at all my pennies, and then looked at this single small green slip of paper he was offering me, in my childlike mindset, I thought that he was trying to trick me so I said no.

As much as my grandfather tried to explain it to me I just didn't get it. I didn't want to let go of my pennies. I didn't know that what he had for me was worth more and far better than what I had. I don't remember now what happened to the jar of pennies or if I ever ended up exchanging it for the twenty dollar bill, but I do know that if I had taken it at that moment, I would've had more money and I wouldn't have had to waste more time collecting pennies trying to reach twenty dollars. So, what's the moral of the story? Don't delay yourself holding onto something just because you think you won't get something better if you let it go.

Many years later I found myself battling with the decision of having to let go once again. It was one of the most difficult decisions I'd have to make up until that point in my life. Mostly because my mind and my heart were in a constant state of war and held me back from being able to let go. This step in the process may have taken me even longer to get through than any other step in the letting go process because there was so much thinking involved.

Making life-altering decisions is difficult. You ask yourself questions like, "Is this the right thing to do?" or "What's going to happen after I make the decision?" and "Who will be affected by my choices?" There is a lot of consideration that goes into it. For some it may only take a matter of months. For others, especially when the heart is involved in the decision-making process, it may take years. In my case, it did take years to arrive at my decision of letting go. So I will try to take you through some of my thought process in order to help facilitate you in your decision-making as well.

One of the first battles I had was trying to figure out if making the decision to let go was actually God's will. This is extremely important. If you are debating on letting go or not, God's input matters and it matters a lot. Although you should take your happiness into consideration when making this decision (which I will discuss later in this chapter) you also must consider if this is what God desires for you. If it is not God's desire for you to let go, then letting go will only cause you more pain and suffering than holding on. So how do you know if this is what God wants? Well I'm glad you asked, because that's exactly what I want to help you figure out next.

In my process of letting go I came across an article by Pastor Chris Russel titled, "How to Make Right Decisions". Pastor Russell encourages the reader to ask themselves thirteen questions when faced with making difficult decisions. I will not share all thirteen questions in this book but I do encourage you to look up this article online and take some time to really think about these questions. I will share some of the questions that really impacted my decision-making process.

One of the questions that I asked myself was what did the Bible have to say about this? Most times, because we are unaware of what the Bible says about a subject, we are easily swayed by doctrines and teachings that have no Biblical foundation. You must know your Bible in order to use it to instruct your life.

If you've never read it or don't own one, there are many free versions online. If you need help interpreting it, seek the counsel of a trusted pastor.

Speaking of trusted pastors brings me to the second question I asked myself. What do my spiritual advisors tell me about this? When making tough decisions most of us tend to turn to someone we trust to gain their input. If you want to hear Godly advice, you need to turn to someone who demonstrates the fruits of God in their life. When I spoke to each of my spiritual advisors, the answer across the board was yes, it's best if you let go. Sometimes the people in our lives will give us advice that doesn't help. Ask yourself, are they connected to God? Can they really give me advice based on God's desire for me?

I also asked myself how this would affect me spiritually? Spiritually I was going down a dark path. I was pulling further and further away from God because of what I was going through, and that was one of the things that made me realize, *this isn't what God wants for me.* Would staying in your situation draw you closer to God or pull you away from Him?

Another question that struck me was if I was paying attention to the risks associated with making the decision to stay instead of letting go. The reality of my situation was that I was running more risk by staying in it than I was by leaving. Would leaving be painful? Yes. But staying would have been detrimental.

The last question that really sealed the deal for me was, do I have peace from God about this? Now the Bible teaches us that the peace that God gives us is not like the peace of the world (John 14:27). It also describes that peace as the peace that surpasses all understanding (Philippians 4:7). Meaning that even when the circumstance looks difficult and even when the decision is difficult, God can still give you peace about making it.

That peace is God's way of giving you security that you are making the right decision. When I made the decision to let go, I felt peace about my decision. I knew that it would be painful, I knew it would be hard, but I had peace in knowing that God was giving me the "okay" to move forward. He was with me, so it didn't matter who didn't agree with my decision.

I will add one more question here that was not in Pastor Russell's article. Up until now we've discussed the question, "how do we know it's God's will to let go?" But a good portion of the answer to that question comes when you ask yourself the following question,

"Was it God's will for you to get into that situation to begin with?" What were the circumstances surrounding your decision to become involved in the situation? Were you being led by God at the time that you made the decision to get involved? Did you seek Godly counsel when you were making that decision? If you did, who did you seek it from? In retrospect, does that person actually demonstrate the fruits of walking with God? Or did they advise you based on their own agenda and perspective? As I said before, there is a lot of thinking to do and lots of questions to ask yourself. But tough decisions require tough analyzation.

When I was seeking advice, one of the people I spoke to during that time was my aunt. I remember having a heartfelt conversation with my aunt about a time when she had to make a decision to let go. During that conversation my aunt passed on some words of wisdom that my grandmother had given her.

My grandmother was a woman of God who had passed away many years ago, but those words she spoke to my aunt surpassed her life and made it into mine, and now I'd like to share them with you. My grandmother said to my aunt, "in life sometimes you will need to make decisions. Never make decisions in order to please others. Make decisions that will lead towards your happiness. Only then will you be at peace and find happiness". This idea of being happy despite others' opinions would continue to recur in my mind for years to come.

I remember that during that time in which I was still contemplating if I should let go or not, my mom would also try to reach out to me and give me advice. She would often ask me if I was happy in my situation, and even though my mind would be screaming no, my lips would always say yes. Although my mom knew better, she would let it go and just continue to pray for me. But in my heart that question, "Are you happy?" would continue to bother me. So as I ask you this same question, I want you to be honest with yourself, "Are you happy?"

The reality is that even if you know that God wants you to let go, sometimes it's still tough to make the decision. In order to actually let go, this is one of those questions you need to honestly ask yourself. God didn't call us to live a life of depression and sadness. In fact a life lived in the presence of God should be filled with joy and eternal pleasures (Psalm 16:11). This does not mean that we will not go through difficulties or tribulations, but according to what the Word says, those moments of sadness and pain are usually temporary (Ecclesiastes 3:4, Psalm 30:5) and God wants to get you out of those seasons of sadness (Psalm 30:11, Jeremiah 29:11). But despite the fact that many who are struggling to let go know that they are unhappy, there is still a very real battle that is going on inside. There are things that will still make us hesitate about letting go.

While there can be many things that keep us from letting go, it seems that the first and foremost thing that prevents us is ourselves. Your mind and your heart are in a constant battle. Your mind tells you to let go, but your heart is telling you not to. It's like a tug-of-war between the heart and mind. Society tells you to follow your heart. But what does that even mean? What heart is society talking about? The heart society is referring to is your emotions and how you feel. But Jeremiah 17:9 states that *"the heart is deceitful above all things"* (a lesson I've learned the hard way).

That's why I want to add here that seeking your happiness is not more important than doing the will of God for your life. The will of God will always lead you to good things even when you have to go through difficult seasons. The Word says that everything works for the good of those who love God and have been called according to His purpose (Romans 8:28). Following God will never lead you to destruction. But to follow your heart, or to seek the happiness of your heart, can lead you astray because the heart is deceitful. Your happiness is important so long as it is aligned with God's will for your life. Outside of Him any pleasure we find will be temporary. The emotions and feelings of the heart can be deceptive in what they want from one moment to the next. But the Bible also mentions the heart in another way.

Proverbs 23:7 provides us with some insight. It states, *"for as a man thinks in his heart so is he"*. We have been taught that the heart feels and the mind thinks. But this verse is talking about the heart thinking. It sounds like a contradiction but it's not. The word heart in this verse refers to the soul; the soul is made up of your thoughts, experiences and emotions. But that word "thinks" is what really got me. The word thinks in Hebrew is "shaar" which literally means to split, open or act as a gatekeeper. Now stay with me, a gatekeeper is someone who controls access to what goes in or out. To summarize, what this verse is really saying is that what you allow to enter into your soul is what you will be.

What does that have to do with holding yourself

back? Well a lot actually because if you have *allowed* yourself to think and believe that you either deserve to be or cannot remove yourself from the situation that you are in, then you will continue to *be* in that situation.

For those of us who struggle with toxic relationships, emotional abuse is often part of the equation. Some of the signs of an emotionally abusive person are possessiveness, explosive tempers, and extreme jealousy. Other signs are that they constantly belittle you, try to isolate you from family and friends, and make false accusations about you (break the cycle, 2018). These are just some, but if you are in this kind of situation it can also quickly escalate into physical abuse. On a side note, there are so many resources for women in abusive situations. If you don't know how to leave, there are places in your community that can and will help you. Don't be afraid to speak out. There is always a way out.

An abuser will use words and can even escalate to physical violence to scar you emotionally and make you believe that you are less valuable than you really are. Those same words and actions will convince you that you can't do this, that you can't let go, and that you can't move on. But you need to get tired of downing yourself and thinking that you can't.

I remember that someone once asked me, Sasha, how did you do it? What they meant was how did I manage to make the decision to leave, and my response was simple, "I got fed up". The reality of the situation was that I had left and returned to the relationship I was in many times. But something in me changed the last time I left. I didn't cry, I didn't get angry, I didn't try to explain myself; I just got tired of it. I got fed up, and let me tell you that's a scary thing, because that is the point of no return. When a woman is fed up with something, there is no changing her mind. Maybe you aren't ready to let go just yet. Maybe you're not quite fed up yet. In fact, research tells us that for women in abusive relationships it can take an average of seven attempts before they finally leave their abuser (Buel). But if nothing changes in your situation, at one point the day will come when you will get fed up and then you will need this book more than ever.

But let us continue. Many of those who took the survey I sent out for this book responded in the same way I did when answering, what caused them to finally let go. We got fed up! In my case, I became tired of living in a way that I knew I didn't deserve to be living.

But I only knew that I didn't deserve it when I chose to see myself the way that God saw me.

I realized that if I am a daughter of the King of Kings and Creator of the universe then I should not be living a depressed, mediocre, and stagnant life. If 1 Peter 2:9 says that I am part of a chosen race, a royal priesthood, a holy nation, a people for God's own possession, that I may proclaim the excellencies of Him who called me out of darkness and into His marvelous light, then why was I living in darkness?

Can I testify a little right now? I was in such a dark place that I would say to God, "just take me, I don't want to live this life anymore, not like this". At times I'd have suicidal thoughts. I would be driving down the highway and would think to myself "what if I just ran this car off the road and ended it". I say this with no filter because I need you to understand the level of darkness that was surrounding my life. I was so depressed that I desired death more than letting go of that which had me in that depressed state. I was listening to my "heart", meaning my emotions, and my emotions were being influenced by negativity. My emotions were telling me it's too hard to let go. My emotions were telling me, death is the only way out. My emotions had caused me to lose sight of my identity.

But the day I got fed up I said no more. That day I decided that I would no longer live under a cloud of depression and self-pity and that I would do something about my situation because this was not what God called me to. I tell you right now, whatever it is that you haven't let go of, whatever it is that is toxic and poisoning your life, you are there by choice. You put yourself there, now it's time to put on your big girl pants and make the decision to get yourself out. I don't mean to sound harsh but I want to be blunt enough to let you know that you have the power to do something about it.

With that being said, if you are in a place of darkness where you are contemplating suicide and feel like you can't get yourself out on your own, talk to someone. Talk to God, talk to a friend, talk to a doctor, a counselor, talk to anyone, but speak up. Your life is worth something. Jesus Christ died on the cross so that you could live, because He loved you that much. You have something to live for. Yourself! You are valuable to God and your life is a part of His beautiful purpose. Don't let the enemy deceive you into throwing your life away. If there is no one you feel safe talking to, then call a suicide hotline. Here's the number for the National Suicide Prevention Hotline: 1-800-273-8255. Don't ever think that there's nothing more you can do. Even now God's hand is reaching out to save you.

I believe that on many occasions God's hand reached out to me and saved me. There were many times when I felt there was no escape to the situation I was in and where I would feel God's presence consoling me and letting me know He was still with me. Having a relationship with God was key in making this decision. Knowing that He was backing up my decision made the difference. Our own thoughts get in the way and don't allow us to hear what God has to say about a situation. For the longest time I thought there was no way out because my mind was focused on how I got in the mess to begin with.

There were so many times I would fill my mind with thoughts of regret, wishing that I had never made certain decisions. It's so easy to think about what we could've done differently in the past, but we don't think about what we can do differently right now. Instead of the "shoulda-woulda-coulda's" why don't you start saying "I will" and "I can"? There was a point in your life before you latched onto this thing, in which you were perfectly fine. That's why we like to say, "if I could go back I'd do things differently". We want to go back to when we were fine, to before the fact. But the truth is that if you were fine before the fact, you can and will be fine after the fact. Time moves forward.

I know that you have been through a lot and maybe you feel like you are damaged goods. But the fact is that everything you've been through hasn't ruined you, it's made you more resilient. If life has beat you up and you're still standing, guess what? That just shows how much tougher you are than your opponent.

This brings to mind a song by Deleon Richards called "Here in me". Part of the chorus says, "You tried to break me, make me believe that I can't, it's too late, I already see myself winning". This song impacted me in a deep way because in my season of letting go I realized that I needed to SEE myself overcoming before I could overcome because I knew that if I believed it, nothing was going to stop me. You need to see yourself winning, you need to see yourself letting go, and you need to believe that you can do it, before you are actually able to do it. That is called faith!

The Bible says in Lamentations 3:51 that the eye affects the heart. That means that what you see with your eyes is what you will believe in your heart, and as

What you allow to enter
into your soul
is what you will be.

Proverbs 23:7 states, what you believe is what you will be. If you start to believe that you will be free, then you will become free.

After you overcome the first obstacle that holds you back (yourself), then you will be ready to overcome the next obstacle, Laban. If you recall from the story earlier, Laban is Rebekah's brother. When Abraham's servant explains to Laban and Bethuel (Rebekah's Father) about how God granted him favor on this journey to find a wife for Isaac, both Laban and Bethuel's responses are unanimous. They say the following, "*The thing has come from the Lord; we cannot speak to you bad or good. Behold, Rebekah is before you; take her and go, and let her be the wife of your master's son, as the Lord has spoken*" (Genesis 24:50-52).

Originally they are both on board with this plan. However, only 4 verses later (the next morning) when Abraham's servant is ready to leave with Rebekah, Laban and his mother say, "Let the young woman remain with us a while, at least ten days; after that she may go". Yet, when Rebekah is asked what she wants to do she decides to go right away (smart girl).

Later in Rebekah's life she is forced to send her favorite son, Jacob, away into hiding. She sends him back to her homeland to her brother Laban. There Jacob falls in love with Laban's daughter Rachel and he asks Laban to marry her. Laban agrees to let him marry Rachel if Jacob will work for him for seven years. Jacob is so in love with Rachel that he agrees to do this.

However, on the morning after his wedding night Jacob realizes that he's been tricked into marrying Leah, Rachel's older sister. When he confronts Laban about this, Laban tells Jacob that it is not the custom to marry off the younger sister before the older and that if he still wants to marry Rachel he will have to work another seven years for him. Jacob agrees once again.

So what am I getting at besides the fact that Laban is a sneaky guy? Laban is a purpose-delayer. Laban is the kind of person who shows up to stop you from making decisions that need to be made that will directly impact your purpose. "Labans" operate by trying to keep you in the same monotonous and unfruitful season that you are in and they show up precisely to prevent or delay you from letting go.

Sometimes Laban is the person or thing you're having a hard time letting go of. Beware of the "Labans" in your life! They are disguised with the attractive clothing of having your best interest at heart but I pray that God will open your spiritual eyes that you will see them and weed them out. These are toxic people and your inability to remove them from your path will hinder you from letting go. So do yourself a favor, tell that Laban in your life, "I am making my decision and I don't need your permission!"

What I do want to point out is Rebekah's unwillingness to be delayed. Her family wasn't telling her not to go. They were just asking for a little more time before she left. But Rebekah didn't fall into the trap. Our problem is that we often do fall into this trap of procrastination in disguise, holding off the inevitable.

But how much longer are you willing to waste away your life? Think about the situation you are in and how you will feel if you're still in it one year from now, or five years from now. What about ten or twenty years? What about always? Are you willing to continue living like this for the rest of your life? And if you have children, are you willing to continue teaching them through your example that this is the correct way to go through life? If you procrastinate for too long, ten days can easily become a lifetime.

Don't turn a lifetime of potential purpose and happiness into a

Beware of the "Labans" in your life... your inability to remove them from your path is directly linked to your inability to let go.

of lifetime of depression and procrastination. You are only given one life to live, live

it wisely. This book is vital to the season that you're in, it has been placed in your hands for such a time as this. It is an invitation to let go of that which is hindering you. Like me, maybe you've asked God to rescue you, one too many times.

Maybe you've been waiting for Him to do something. Well today I tell you, He has heard you. So if you were waiting for a sign, this might be it. I leave you with 2 Corinthians 6:2:

"For He [God] says: 'In an acceptable time I have heard you, and in the day of salvation I have helped you.' Behold, now is the accepted time; behold, now is the day of salvation."

Questions for Reflection:

1. What are the things in yourself that are holding you back?

2. What have you allowed yourself to think and believe about your situation?

3. Are you seeing yourself the way God sees you? If not, why and what can you do to change that?

4. Who are the "Labans" in your life?

5. What can you do to free yourself from their influence?

6. What positive things would you be doing with your life if you weren't in this situation?

Notes:

_____

_____

_____

_____

_____

_____

_____

_____

_____

_____

_____

_____

_____

_____

_____

_____

_____

_____

_____

_____

_____

_____

Prayer

My Heavenly Father,

I present to You my sister. Right now she is battling with having to let go. I pray that You open her spiritual eyes that she may see the obstacles that are impeding her from being able to let go. Give her wisdom to overcome her own conflicted emotions, and courage to separate herself from the "Labans" in her life.

I declare that she is Yours and that Your purpose will be fulfilled in her despite any obstacles in her way.

In the name of Jesus, Amen.

-Chapter Five-
SHE WILL KNOT
BE BITTER

She is clothed with strength and dignity;
she can laugh at the days to come."
—Proverbs 31:25

This chapter is for the woman who wasn't given the opportunity to make the decision to let go. Up until this point I've discussed having the courage to come to the decision to let go. Maybe you thought about letting go, but before you could come to that decision, it was made for you. Maybe you are struggling to let go of a person who passed away. That doesn't make it any less difficult. In fact, I'd dare to say it's more difficult to let go when it's not your choice to begin with.

So where do we go from here? We go forward. We take it one step at a time, one day at a time, one moment at a time, one tear at a time; but we move forward. In the next chapter of this book I discuss entering your "desert season" which I refer to as the emotional part of the letting go process.

Before this point I've only discussed coming to the decision of physically separating yourself from the situation, and as hard as that may sound, it's not the hardest part of letting go. The emotional part is the hard part, and if you were let go of, then you were just thrown into your desert season with no preparation and no time to plan. But I want to meet you right where you're at.

Although I was the one who made the decision to let go in my situation, I can't help but think how things might have been different if the other person involved hadn't left me alone for a few days. In those few days they were gone I felt so many mixed emotions. I was sad, I was embarrassed, I felt empty, I felt rejected, and I was so angry. I wanted to teach them a lesson. I wanted them to regret what they had done.

But underneath all that anger, really all I wanted was for them to come back and love me. I so deeply desired to be loved, to be cared for, and to be appreciated. I felt so angry because I had given this person another chance to resolve the situation and they decided to leave when what I wanted was for them to stay. I know that many times as women we don't want to show our true emotions, and in fact, what we end up doing is hiding our pain and hurt with bitterness and anger. Even if we use those things to protect us, they are not a long term cure for the real problem.

We can't put a Band-Aid over a fatal wound and think it will resolve it. A wound left untreated will only become infected over time. Contrary to popular belief, time does not heal all wounds. Anger and bitterness can function like a Band-Aid over a wound of hurt, shame, and rejection. But without properly treating the wound, it will only make our process of letting go that much more difficult and painful.

In fact, what can end up happening when we don't deal with anger and bitterness properly is that we can hurt other people. Have you ever heard that saying, "hurt people, hurt people"? If we don't move quickly to deal with our own hurts, we will end up hurting people close to us, and in the long run we will also damage future relationships. I know it's easier said than done, but that Band-Aid can only cover that wound up for so long before it gets infected.

Things like asking yourself repeatedly why they left you, or what you could have done differently won't change anything now. The fact is what's done is done and we can't move the hands of time backwards. As I said before all we can do now is go forward. So you have this hurt, this anger, this bitterness, and these questions. What do you do with them? Bring them to God. Be sincere and just tell Him how you feel.

I remember one time wanting to talk to someone about something I was going through but no one was available. I felt so discouraged because I really needed to get this thing off my chest. But then I heard the voice of God in my spirit saying "just talk to Me". So I began bluntly telling God what I was going through and I must have cried for a good twenty minutes, but after that I felt better. I felt like I had unloaded something off of my shoulders and placed it in God's hands. It was exactly what I needed and it's probably what you need to. So, bring Him all these mixed feelings and emotions. I'll repeat what He said to me, just talk to Him. He's waiting to lend an ear.

In the meantime, let's address that anger. Surprisingly, anger used correctly can actually be beneficial. The Bible says in Ephesians 4:26-27 *"Be angry and do not sin, do not let the sun go down on your wrath, nor give place to the devil."* It is not a sin to be angry, but if you allow anger to overtake you, it can cause you to sin. You must direct your anger to the right person.

According to Ephesians 6:12, your battle is not against flesh and blood, it is against the powers of this dark world and against the spiritual forces of evil. When you get angry at people for what they've done to you or for leaving you behind, and you allow that anger to continue day in and day out, it becomes bitterness. It becomes hatred and lack of forgiveness, and when you allow these things to enter your heart, you give the devil a foothold over you.

Now that word "foothold" is very interesting because it literally means a hold for the feet. It makes me think of Genesis 3:15 when God is punishing the serpent for enticing Eve into sinning by eating the forbidden fruit. God speaks to the serpent and says, *"I will put enmity between you and the woman, and between your offspring and hers; he will crush your head and you will strike his heel"* (Genesis 3:15). There's that reference to the foot (or heel) again. We have a real enemy and there is enmity (or hostility) between us. He will always try to cause us to stumble by making us do what God has already instructed us not to do, and then by causing us to be angry at that thing instead of him.

Ladies, by nature we are emotional beings and the enemy knows that. Don't let that be your downfall. Let us not waste time being angry with someone, when our real enemy is running free, laughing and scheming against us. The best thing that could have happened to me, was that this person left for a few days. It was in those few days that I was able to have some clarity. It was in those days that I diverted my attention and turned my anger towards my real enemy.

It's easy to blame the person or blame God, but we have to remember that we live in a fallen world. The Bible says that the devil is the prince of this world (Ephesians 2:2). Yet, its fallen state is not God's doing. But at the moment that I came to my senses and realized who my real enemy was, it was then that I decided that I would not let this thing tear me down.

Right then and there I decided that I would hold my head up high, that I would forgive even if it was the hardest thing I'd ever have to do. I would get myself back up, and I would fight for me. I would fight for my dignity. I would fight for my self-worth. I would fight for my happiness, because even though I wasn't happy now, I did deserve to be. I had decided that I would not stop fighting until I had achieved it all.

I would not let fear of being alone paralyze me when I serve a God who says that He will never leave me or forsake me (Hebrews 13:5). I would not let the thought of the amount of time I had wasted or would never get to have, keep me from achieving my dreams when my times are in His hands (Psalm 31:15). I would not let low self-esteem and depression keep me from shining and being myself when the very son of God (the Creator of the universe) shed His blood for me just to prove how much I was worth to Him (John 3:16).

I decided not to let my anger turn me bitter. Instead I allowed anger to be the impulse to make me better. There is something better waiting for you at the end of this process, and by better I mean better than the place you are in now, because there is life after this.

Nothing can replace what you had, but you can have new things moving forward. The only catch is you have to believe it. You have to believe that God's plans for your future are for good (Jeremiah 29:11). You have to believe that your best days are not behind you but ahead of you. I know it's hard to believe when past experience seems to tell you the opposite, but faith is about believing even when you cannot see. Make this your new motto, *"I am clothed with strength and dignity, I can laugh at the days to come"* (Proverbs 31:25). Better days will come, and God will not allow you to walk through this desert alone. This book that you're reading is proof of that already. Help is on the way!

But as long as you continue to be angry you will delay your process and you will delay the better things that God has in store for you. So, no, maybe it wasn't your decision to physically let go and separate yourself from the person, but it is your decision to let go emotionally and free yourself from the captivity of anger, bitterness and resentment. You may not know it yet, but maybe, being let go of is the best thing that's ever happened to you. Either way if you're ready to start letting go in your heart, then read on, you have just entered your desert season.

Questions for Reflection:

1. What are some of the feelings you may be hiding under bitterness and anger?

2. What can you do to acknowledge those feelings in a healthy way?

3. What fears are you allowing to paralyze you?

4. What are the specific things you are angry about?

5. How can you use that anger in a positive way?

Notes:

_____

_____

_____

_____

_____

_____

_____

_____

_____

_____

_____

_____

_____

_____

_____

_____

_____

_____

_____

Prayer

Father,

I pray for the woman who wasn't able to make the decision to let go. Lord, console her in her time of hurt and help her to acknowledge those feelings of pain so that she may deal with them appropriately. Do not allow her heart to be filled with bitterness but give her the strength to overcome. Help her to become better and to come out of this with hope for the future. Be with her now Lord, even as she may be feeling a mix of negative emotions. Let her know that nothing she feels can separate her from Your love. Heal her and help her to continue this process of letting go.

In the name of Jesus, Amen.

-Chapter Six-

SHE WILL NOT CLING TO THE FAMILIAR:
PART 1 OF THE DESERT SEASON

"It is written, 'Man shall not live by bread alone, but by every word that proceeds from the mouth of God.'"
—Matthew 4:4

STEP 3: PHYSICAL DETACHMENT

So you've finally made the decision to let go, now what? Well, now you finish letting go. If you've decided to let go and have separated yourself from the situation or person that was keeping you down, then I'm sure by now you've figured out that it's much harder to do than you thought.

Letting go is a two part process, it is as much a physical process as it is an emotional one. Since you have now chosen to separate yourself from the thing that was suffocating you, a change in your environment is necessary. But making that change of environment and keeping it will be difficult. The physical aspect of letting go is the literal removal of yourself from the situation. In order to remove yourself and stay removed, you must set boundaries.

Without boundaries you will inescapably fall back into the hands of that which had you tied up. So how do you set those boundaries? Let's begin by trying to understand what a boundary is and what it's meant to do. A boundary is something that indicates a limit. The purpose of a boundary in this situation is to protect yourself from others and from yourself. At this point in the letting go process there are tough decisions you have to make that no one else can make for you, and if you aren't careful, your feelings and emotions will keep you from making them.

This is why one of the first things you must do upon removing yourself from a person or situation is to set limits between you and them so that you are not yanked back into the mess all over again. If you fail to set boundaries, you will inevitably remain bound. You will continue to be knotted and tangled up in the situations you've fought so hard to get out of. There are just some people who are not meant to go into your next season with you and if you don't set limits on them, they will come along for the ride uninvited. I'll share a few things I did to set boundaries for myself after letting go of my relationship.

One way to set limits and boundaries with certain people is to cut communication with them. This means phone calls, texting, and even social media. The best way to do so without disrespecting people is to just let them know you need some time for yourself and you need some space. Another way to help set boundaries is by changing up your routine. For example, if you're use to going to the same coffee shop and you know you're going to run into people there, then find another coffee shop to go to. If it's a habit or situation you need to set boundaries with, then avoid being in places

If you fail to set boundaries,

you will inevitably

remain bound.

where the temptation to get involved again might arise.

A third way to set boundaries is to stop posting personal things about your life on social media. You want to limit access to your life so that you can have the freedom to make tough decisions, free of people's negative opinions and judgment. The last thing you need is people coming into your desert season and trying to convince you to go back into bondage. With social media also comes the danger of viewing things you shouldn't be seeing, such as photos and videos that might trigger emotions and desires. RED FLAG! That's the quickest way to fall back. Boundaries are not just for other people they are also for you.

If you're letting go of a relationship like I am, then be careful of the type of music you are listening to. You might have to put boundaries on your music as well. Love songs are probably not what you want to be listening to after a break up. Nor do you want to be listening to music that is going to make you angry all over again. Do yourself a favor, set some boundaries in your desert season, otherwise you may never make it out.

There's also a book called, "Boundaries" by Doctors Henry Cloud and John Townsend that I believe can really be helpful in equipping you to learn to establish boundaries. Something I discovered about myself during my process of letting go was that I had to set boundaries in other areas of my life as well. I had in past times been too quick to say yes, I was quick to take on more responsibilities and more tasks. When it came to the relationship I had let go of, I had taken on more nonsense than I needed to.

My failure to set boundaries early on in that relationship was part of the reason why I ended up knotted up in it in the first place. Boundaries ladies, I can't stress it enough. They are necessary when letting go, but also in every other aspect of life. I definitely recommend the book. It may be a life-changer for you.

STEP 4: EMOTIONAL DETACHMENT

Now as you detach from what was hindering you, things may begin to feel different. While you may have physically separated yourself from the situation when you decided to let go, or were let go of, your emotions will take some time to catch up. I'm sure that when Rebekah had to let go of her family to go to a new and mysterious land, she must have been filled with mixed emotions. As clear cut as her decision to leave was, I'm sure it must have saddened her to let go of her situation. When Rebekah left home she had to embark on a long journey through the desert to arrive at Canaan where her future husband lived.

I imagine that Rebekah's journey through the desert, surrounded by people she didn't know, might have stirred up some feelings in her. That time in the desert might have stirred up feelings of loneliness, sadness, fear, and doubt of whether she had made the right decision. These are the same feelings you will face after you physically let go and enter into, what I like to call, the desert season.

The desert season is the second part of the letting go process, the emotional detachment. I like the analogy of the desert because it implies loneliness, and the idea of deserting something gives the implication of leaving something behind. The desert feels empty, it feels lonely, and it feels scary. After I physically let go, I entered into my desert season. I felt lonely because I was no longer around the person I had let go of, and I was afraid because I had no idea where I was going or what I was going to face in that desert.

Many times I contemplated going back. It was still an option realistically, but I had to have enough faith and boldness to face the fear of the unknown. There was comfort in having knowledge of what I was leaving behind because at least I knew what I'd be getting into if I ever went back. But the memory of why I left, pushed me further into this desert of the unknown.

Many times after we make the decision to let go and we are left with the empty feeling of the unknown it seems like the best decision is to go back. But if you were anything like me, then you've gone back before, and going back has only proven that leaving was always the better option. Do not cling to the familiar for the sake of comfort. It is a web of lies that we ourselves spin for fear of entering the desert of the unknown.

The desert will strip you of comfort. It will challenge you so much that you will yearn to go back. But do not fret, there is good news yet. God will not abandon you in the midst of your desert season. In fact, often times God will send people to help you through that desert season.

Finding Your Support Network

For Rebekah there were two kinds of people that went on her journey through the desert. The first were her maids. These were people who had been with her in her past situation but who were also willing to travel into her new season with her without holding her back. You need people like this in your life who will remind you of where God brought you out of. These are people who truly have your best interest at heart and who will not stop you from going to where God leads you, but will be willing to take the journey with you. They are a strong emotional support.

The other group of people that traveled with Rebekah were Abraham's servants. They were not a part of Rebekah's past but they knew the way to Rebekah's future. You will also need these people in your desert season. They are the people God has chosen to share the vision for your life with and they will help get you there. They will show up when you least expect it and usually when you most need them. This is the combination of people that God will use to help you transition from your last season to your next season. They will be there through your desert season.

These people are what many might call your support network. One of the questions I asked in the survey I sent out was about what things helped women in their process of letting go. Just about half of the women surveyed said that having a strong support network was what helped them remain firm on their decision to let go. The other popular reason women stated, was that their desire to better themselves helped them stand firm on the decision. The purpose of your support network is just that, to help support you as you better yourself.

A support network is basically a group of people you can turn to when you are going through a difficult moment. The Bible advises us to have people we can turn to in our time of need in Ecclesiastes 4:9-10 (ESV) which states, *"Two are better than one, because they have a good reward for their toil. For if they fall, one will lift up his fellow. But woe to him who is alone when he falls and has not another to lift him up!"* Your support network's job is to lift you up during this difficult time of letting go. In fact in this verse, the Bible warns of the dangers of not having a support when you are in the lows of life.

I remember that throughout my whole process of letting go God began to connect me to different women who showed up precisely when I needed them. These women united with me in my time of need to help me with things like shelter, money, advice, support, and even legal help. I don't believe I would have made it without God using these women to come together and help me in my time of need. Never in my life had I witnessed female solidarity in such a way. I urge you to seek your support network during this time. They will be a vital part of your letting go process. Don't try to do this alone.

My support network was made up of friends, family, my counselor, my pastors, my church family and even some co-workers. I tried to surround myself with people who were like-minded, people who were a positive influence, and who I knew had my best interest at heart. These were people who wanted to push me forward and motivate me to do better.

If you don't have a good support network, letting go will be that much harder. Now if you don't feel comfortable confiding in people, then I definitely recommend finding a *good* counselor in your area (emphasis on the word "good"). Do your research when it comes to this. For me it was important to have a counselor who was a believer like me and who could understand my beliefs when counseling me. The upside of a counselor is that they are separated enough from your situation to advise you without any biases.

Another option is to find support groups in your community. Support groups can be helpful because they connect you to other people who are going through the same situation. It allows you to be able to have empathy with each other and be supportive of each other's processes. Family can also be an important addition to a support network because for the most part they are on your team (although I know this is not always the case). This brings me to finding support within the church.

A church can be much like a second family, a home away from home. This can be one of the greatest additions to your support network. I know my pastors and church family were for me. However, when it comes to finding a good church, again, do your research. If you already have a great church that supports you, stay there and allow yourself to be loved on and helped through this process.

However, if you don't have a church or if you are in a church that is not supporting you or trying to lift you up in your time of need then I suggest you try finding a church that does try to build you up. If you're not ready for all that, then I suggest you pray to God about it. The Bible says, *"ask and it will be given to you, seek and you shall find"* (Matthew 7:7 NIV). If you ask God to bring you people that will help and support you through this process, He will do it.

I also want to point out that a support network doesn't have to be a large group of people with a broad variety of qualities. In fact your focus when building this network should be on the quality of the people in your circle as opposed to the amount of people. As cliché as it may sound, sometimes less really is more.

There are some specific qualities that people in my support network had that I believe are essential for those who will be supporting you through this process. I found that the following seven qualities could be found in my support network:

1. Trust

2. Honesty

3. Prior experience letting go

4. An Unbiased Opinion

5. Unconditional Love

6. Wise Advice

7. Encouragement

Trust- Trust is one quality that everyone in your support network should have. Someone who supports you will not betray your trust by sharing information that you have confided to them. Proverbs 17:9 (ESV) states that *"whoever covers an offense seeks love, but he who repeats a matter separates close friends."* It's vital that you be able to confide in the people in your support network. It is only through talking about what you're going through, that the situation and emotions surrounding it begin to lose power over you. With that being said, it's important that those things you share remain between you and the people you choose to share them with. Otherwise, as the verse states, loose information can separate close friends.

Honesty- Proverbs 27:5 (ESV) *"Better is open rebuke than hidden love."* Having honest people in your circle is important during this season of letting go because through this process, at times, your own feelings and emotions will get in the way of you being able to see the reality of a situation. A friend who truly loves you, will be honest with you and correct or confront you when you need it.

Prior experience letting go- There are two reasons why you should have at least one person in your inner circle who has prior experience with letting go. One reason is that you need someone who has literally been in your shoes to be able to empathize with you and truly understand what you are going through. The Bible says in Hebrews 4:15 (NIV) when speaking of

Jesus that *"we do not have a high priest who is unable to empathize with our weaknesses, but we have one who has been tempted in every way, just as we are--yet he did not sin."* Jesus is able to empathize with us because He became human like us and literally stepped into our shoes in order to understand our weaknesses and overcome them as a human Himself. Likewise, someone who is able to empathize with you because they have been through something similar is valuable as a part of your support network because they can understand and support you on a level that other people may not be able to.

Secondly, Luke 6:39 (ESV) states, *"Can a blind man lead a blind man? Will they not both fall into a pit?"* What this means is that if someone does not have the prior experience or knowledge to guide you out of something, it is likely that you will both fail. So, it's important to have someone who's gone through the process of letting go and successfully moved on so that they can guide you in doing so as well.

<u>Unbiased opinion-</u> As I stated previously, the perks of having a counselor for me was that she was able to offer me an unbiased opinion. She was not emotionally tied to the situation so she was able to see the situation from an outside perspective and offer me

impartial advice. Romans 2:11 (ESV) teaches us that *"God shows no partiality."* This means He has no biased or unfair opinion when it comes to His children. He sees things from an outside perspective and can direct us and guide us through the best course of action because of this. Therefore, an impartial person can make a great addition to your support network.

Unconditional Love- Letting go causes many mixed emotions. Having people around you who love you regardless of your outbursts, your moments of weakness, your tears and happy moments is absolutely necessary. The Bible says in Proverbs 17:17 (ESV) that *"a friend loves at all times, and a brother is born for adversity."* Having people in your network who can love you through the ups and downs of this process will allow you to express even the rawest of your emotions without fear of judgment. These could be family, close friends, pastors, etc.

Wise Advice- Proverbs 27:9 (ESV) states that *"the sweetness of a friend comes from his earnest counsel."* This means that a good friend gives good and sincere advice. This is necessary in a season in which your emotions might guide you to make unwise decisions. Having someone whose counsel you can count on will facilitate the process.

Encouragement- One of the things that I often needed during my process of letting go was someone who would encourage me on the days I was feeling down. These are people in your life who check up on you, who pray for you and who are always willing to say just the right words when you need them. 1 Thessalonians 5:11 (ESV) says that we should _"encourage one another and build one another up..."_ As you are letting go you will need people in your support network to help build you back up.

Having this network of supportive people who were in my corner really helped me to get through some of the roughest parts of the desert season and I believe it can do the same for you. It is always good to be able to lean on someone for support when your own strength is lacking.

However, there is a third group of people I should mention. These are people whom you should NOT allow to be a part of your support network nor should you try to take them with you into your desert season. For Rebekah these were her family. Many times when we let go of people, we still find ways to continue to be attached to them. We may leave the situation but continue to have contact with people involved in the situation. Or we may continue to surround ourselves with people who knew the person we decided to let go of. Doing so, is to tread on dangerous territory. The important thing to remember here is what I said earlier in this chapter, set boundaries, and set them for as long as you feel necessary in order to protect yourself.

With that being said, I do want to remind you that the desert season is not meant to be a permanent place, it is only a season of transition if you allow it to be. But your desert will either make or break you. In the book of Exodus it recounts the story of the people of God and their enslavement in Egypt. Through a process of ten plagues that God sent to Egypt, the Pharaoh finally released the Israelite people, and Moses being led by God, lead the Israelites out of Egypt and into the desert telling them that God would lead them to a Promised Land. The trip from Egypt to Canaan (the Promised Land) should have only taken about eleven days. However, it took the Israelites forty years to finally arrive in the Promised Land of Canaan.

The reason it took the Israelites so long to enter the Promised Land was because in their hearts they were still holding on to the "comforts" of Egypt. Exodus 16:3 demonstrates the complaints of the people and their desire to return to their comfortable state of slavery. *"And the children of Israel said to them, "Oh, that we had died by the hand of the LORD in the land of Egypt, when we sat by the pots of meat and when we ate bread to the full! For you have brought us out into this wilderness to kill this whole assembly with hunger."* The Israelites were so uncomfortable in the desert that they preferred to go back to slavery than to continue moving forward.

When we read this scripture from the outside looking in, it sounds crazy that they would prefer to go back to slavery than to continue their journey through the desert, where at least they were free. But in reading it more closely I realized that the Israelites were doing the same thing that we tend to do when we don't want to let go of something. The Israelites were choosing to remember the good aspects of Egypt, the fact that they were being fed every day. But in their complaint to Moses they failed to recall the part where they were being enslaved and had no freedom.

How many times do we do that? We think back to past relationships or past places and we think of the good memories we had, but we fail to remember the misery that caused us to leave those things in the first place.

I warn you ladies, do not let the discomfort of a temporary season push you back into your season of bondage. Your desert season is not intended to be a long one, but if you continue to emotionally hold on to that which God has already instructed you to let go of, then you will remain stranded in your desert season.

One of the things that helped me to stop having those urges to run back was when I began to break soul ties. Soul ties are most commonly formed through sexual intercourse but they can also be formed through deep friendships and through verbal vows and commitments. They are the knitting together of souls. When there are soul ties, no matter how far you try to pull away from the person you are tied to, your emotions and thoughts will consistently pull you back to them.

The most common reference to soul ties in Scripture is in Mark 10:7-8 which states, *"For this reason a man will leave his father and mother and be united to his wife, and the two will become one"*. The two becoming one is referencing how two souls become knitted together to become one. If we think of this in a literal sense, you have to unknot yourself from that soul tie in order to be able to let go.

Some of the things I did when I broke my soul tie to the person I was letting go of was that I repented of disobeying God by becoming involved with the person.

If there was a sin committed that led to the soul tie, you should repent of it. I also got rid of items that had an emotional tie to the person because those things made it harder for me to let go. If the objects are out of sight and no longer in your possession, it will be easier to keep them out of your mind. I also had to forgive the person for things they had done and I had to forgive myself as well (we will discuss forgiveness in a later chapter). The last thing I did was verbally renouncing to the soul tie and declaring it to be broken in the name of Jesus.

I was able to do these things on my own but if you don't feel comfortable doing so I would talk to a pastor you trust to help you through the process and give you more information on how to break the soul tie. What I can tell you is that breaking the soul tie helped me to speed up my process of emotionally letting go. I don't recommend that you skip this step because doing so might actually prevent you from exiting your desert season for years. The only other way out of the desert is to go back to where you came from. But if you've already figured out that where you came from will only lead to your destruction, then I suggest we continue. We must face this desert.

Do not let the discomfort of a temporary season push you back into your season of bondage.

I remember that one of the things that happened after I let go and entered my desert season was that the residue of that last season was still affecting my lifestyle. All of the hard work I had put into making my situation work had not ceased even after I had left the situation behind me. In an attempt to move past my situation I had gotten a second job. I thought that this would keep me distracted and focused on something other than the pain that letting go had caused me, and for a while it worked. There's nothing wrong with finding something productive to do to keep your mind off your pain. However, don't allow yourself to become so distracted that you avoid dealing with your pain altogether.

So, here I was working two jobs. I would leave one and go to the other. I would come home, go to sleep and do it all over again the next day. By this time, I had moved back in with my mother. She was one of those people that knew my past but was willing to take the journey into my future with me. But something began to happen. I had become so preoccupied and exhausted with the amount of work I was doing that I wasn't taking care of other basic things. I was becoming messy. I wouldn't do my bed in the morning, I'd leave clothes all over the place. I had a mess of

Don't allow yourself to
become so distracted that
you avoid dealing with
your pain.

books, papers, and just stuff in general everywhere.

Eventually my mom took notice. She came to me one day and said, "Sash, your room has been really messy lately. I don't want you to get offended by what I'm about to say but you know, many times the way that someone's living area looks, reflects how they are feeling emotionally as well". I responded with an, "I know mom". I continued, "I just feel like I worked so hard to make sure everything was perfect in my past situation that now I just don't want to do anything. I don't feel like cleaning. I'm overworked and too tired to do anything". My mother responded, "Well, why are you working two jobs?" I said, "Because I need money". My mom replied back, "Well if you need anything I could just buy it for you, you don't need to have two jobs". I replied, "But I don't want you to buy me anything".

"Why not?" my mom asked.

"Because I don't", I stated back.

I began to think about my mom's question, "why not?" Why didn't I want my mom to buy me anything? Why was I so obsessed with providing for myself? Why was I so stuck on not having to depend on anyone? It was because the situation of my past season had molded me to be that way. In my past situation I had to depend on myself financially and I had learned not to trust others when it came to my finances. Often times I had found myself lacking money and being unable to pay for basic needs. In fact, I had even racked up a lot of credit card debt in that season.

Now that I was in a new season, the residue of having to depend on myself was still all over me and it was still affecting me. I had physically separated myself from everything that happened to me, but I was continuing to react as if it was still happening.

The best way I can explain it is by having you imagine that you are the driver in a car. You are so use to driving because you've always had to drive. No one else has ever driven you around. But now all of a sudden, you are in the passenger seat. Someone else is driving and you feel like they are driving to closely to the car in front of them. You begin to get scared and you begin to push your right foot down as if you had a brake petal in front of you.

That's how this felt, as if I was hitting imaginary brakes, because I was so used to doing that action that even when I didn't have to do it anymore, I was still continuing to do it. Many times this is what we do when we come out of a bad situation. It's almost like your mind can't wrap itself around the fact that you are really out of the situation.

It's as if you've been locked in a jail cell for so long, that now that the door is open and you are free, you continue to sit in the jail cell. Feelings of shame, guilt, and sadness will have the same effect on you. But when you begin to place those burdens on God, He will begin to take the weight of those feelings away from you and He will guide you into the bright future He has planned for you.

Eventually, after coming to the realization that my behaviors were out of habit from my past situation, I decided to quit my second job. After that conversation with my mother on that day, I went to church. My mother had decided to stay home that day, and when I returned from church she had cleaned my room for me. Her words to me were, "now that it's clean, keep it that way".

I believe that God used my mom to teach me a valuable lesson that day. He had used her to tell me that I was carrying burdens that He didn't ask me to take on (once again), and that because of these burdens I was neglecting other seemingly insignificant responsibilities that I should have been taking care of. But the fact of the matter was that my mom was right. My room was reflecting the disorder that I still had inside me. I was working with no purpose. I had taken on another job that God didn't ask me to take on and it was affecting my personal and spiritual life, because besides the messy room, I was too tired to even pray or spend time studying the Word of God.

When my mom cleaned my room for me it was the final part of the lesson I needed. God was reminding me, "I got you out of that situation and cleaned up your mess, now keep it clean". Once God brings you out of your situation and helps you to physically let go, don't let the residue of past hurts sneak back into your life and steal your time and purpose away.

When God rescued you, He did it with a purpose. Allow the desert season to process you and lead you to the greater plan God has for your life. Leave the emotional residue of Egypt behind and embrace your desert. God will be with you every step of the way and He is able to guide you because He Himself knows that desert very well.

You see, Jesus was no exception to the desert season. He underwent His own season in the desert. This was His transition season, in which He had to let go of "Jesus the carpenter" and embrace "Jesus the Savior". Jesus spent forty days in the desert before He began His three year ministry that ended in His death by crucifixion (what we now see as His greatest victory and fulfillment of His purpose on earth). In forty days Jesus accomplished a task that took the Israelites forty years to accomplish, He made it through the desert season.

Although the Israelites eventually made it to the Promised Land, it was not the Israelites who were enslaved in Egypt that made it to Canaan, but their children born in the desert who were able to enter the Promised Land. The Israelites who left Egypt were never able to emotionally let go of Egypt, and their inability to let go, left them stranded in the desert until they died. Listen woman, it may be scary not knowing what is to come after letting go, but I can guarantee you of what is to come if you don't. You will either return to Egypt and remain enslaved the rest of your life, or you will remain stranded in the desert like the Israelites until you die there, never reaching your Promised Land.

Fortunately for us, when Jesus entered His desert season He was successful and left us a hint as to how to succeed in this season. Let's take a look at this in Matthew 4:1-11:

Then Jesus was led up by the Spirit into the wilderness to be tempted by the devil. 2 And when

He had fasted forty days and forty nights, afterward He was hungry. **3** Now when the tempter came to Him, he said, "If You are the Son of God, command that these stones become bread."

4 But He answered and said, "It is written, 'Man shall not live by bread alone, but by every word that proceeds from the mouth of God.'"

5 Then the devil took Him up into the holy city, set Him on the pinnacle of the temple, **6** and said to Him, "If You are the Son of God, throw Yourself down. For it is written:

'He shall give His angels charge over you,'

and, 'In their hands they shall bear you up, Lest you dash your foot against a stone.'"

7 Jesus said to him, "It is written again, 'You shall not tempt the LORD your God.'"

8 Again, the devil took Him up on an exceedingly high mountain, and showed Him all the kingdoms of the world and their glory. **9** And he said to Him, "All these things I will give You if You will fall down and worship me."

10 Then Jesus said to him, "Away with you, Satan! For it is written, 'You shall worship the LORD your God, and Him only you shall serve.'"

11 Then the devil left Him, and behold, angels came and ministered to Him. -Matthew 4:1-11 (NKJV)

Three times the devil tempts Jesus. Now here's the thing that people fail to see. The devil can only tempt people with what they already desire. The first thing Jesus is tempted with is turning stones into bread. Jesus had been fasting in the desert for forty days. He was hungry! That's why He was tempted with turning stones into bread. While He certainly had the capacity to make it happen, He didn't. Instead He responded by quoting Scripture. He said, "Man shall not live by bread alone, but by every word that proceeds from the mouth of God". The key to surviving the desert is in this Scripture.

The Scripture Jesus was quoting is from the book of Deuteronomy chapter eight verse three, and it's actually part of a longer verse. The person speaking in Deuteronomy is Moses (the man God used to lead the Israelites out of Egypt) and he is speaking to the Israelites. The full verse reads as follows:

"So He humbled you, allowed you to hunger, and fed you with manna which you did not know nor did your fathers know, that He might make you know that man shall not live by bread alone; but man lives by every word that proceeds from the mouth of the LORD."

So where is the big secret to finally getting past the desert season? The secret is in depending on God and every word He has spoken. Moses explains that God allowed the Israelites to hunger and then fed them with manna (which was bread directly from heaven) so that they would learn to depend on God and the promises He had spoken to them. It is only through depending on God to come through with His promises that we will be able to endure the desert.

Manna in your desert season

The Israelites main complaint was their hunger; and just as they hungered in their desert season, you will too. You will hunger for love, for acceptance, for companionship, and for all the things you had before that were lost when you let go. But just as God provided manna in the desert for the Israelites, He will provide you with all that you need to hold you over until your next season. You may not have what you want now, but you will survive until you arrive where

You may not have what you want now, but you will survive until you arrive where God wants you.

God wants you.

The word "manna" means "what is it?". When God began to send manna from heaven, the Israelites didn't really know what it was at first. Likewise, when God provides you with manna in your desert season you might not recognize it as being manna. But manna is God's provision. For many, letting go comes with the fear that you will not be able to make it on your own. Realistically, when the Israelites left they wouldn't have been able to make it on their own. Had it not been for God's provision they would have starved in the desert.

God will not allow you to starve in your desert. When I made the decision to let go, I knew that it would come with the consequence of being homeless for some time because I could not afford to live on my own. But God's first sign of manna in my life was a beautiful soul that He used to take me in. This woman opened up the doors of her home for me and didn't charge me a dime for the four months that I remained there. God had provided a roof over my head.

Manna is also God's gift. Many times when we make bad decisions that put us into bad predicaments, we end up walking outside of the will of

God and this can block many blessings from coming our way. But once you step back into the will of God, He also begins to send you gifts and good surprises.

I remember that a month after letting go I was able to release my second book titled, "Queen Bees". I didn't have the money or resources to have a book release. I didn't even have the thought in mind to have a book release. But God put it in the heart of the pastor of the church I was visiting, to throw me a book release. She and the women of the church came together and planned and decorated everything. All I had to do was show up. But I was so amazed at how God had given me such a beautiful gift without me having done anything to earn it. The desert season is painful, but even within that pain God sends you provision and He sends you good gifts to get you through it. However, if we don't learn to enjoy the manna God provides in the midst of our wilderness, then we will always see the bad as outweighing the good.

Mirages in the desert

As I write this chapter I am still in my desert season. There were points where I thought that I was done with my desert season, but just this week I realized that I'm not. So beware of mirages in the desert. Merriam Webster dictionary defines a mirage as "an optical effect that is sometimes seen in the desert that may have the appearance of a pool of water..." If you were stranded in an actual desert a mirage would make you think there was water when there actually isn't. In a similar way, there comes a point that you feel so confident that you are emotionally letting go, that you think you're all done with the wilderness season but you actually aren't.

But 1 Corinthians 10:12 reminds us, *"if you think you're standing firm, be careful that you do not fall! (NIV)"* It's important to heed this warning. I was so confident that I was done with this season that when something triggered memories of the past, I became an emotional wreck; and it's okay that this happens. When we find that there are triggers that produce feelings of anger or resentment, it just means we've discovered another area in ourselves that still needs healing and we can now address it and keep moving forward.

As Rebekah pressed forward through her desert, there was a promise attached to the end of that journey. She was leaving her family but she was traveling towards her husband and the promise of a new life. There is also something waiting for you at the end of your desert. Jeremiah 29:11 states: *For I know the plans I have for you," declares the LORD, "plans to prosper you and not to harm you, plans to give you hope and a future."* Although we may not know what's on the other side of the desert, promises like the one in Jeremiah 29:11, remind us that whatever it is, it's going to be good because God's plans for us are good.

So take advantage of your time in the desert. Temptations will come like they did to Jesus, and the desire to go back will haunt you as it did the Israelites. But in those moments remember why you're going through this desert. Don't get caught up in the discomfort of the unknown but instead be humble enough to open yourself up to God and allow Him to reveal to you the areas that are still in need of healing. Remember, this desert may bring up a lot of mixed emotions but it is only for a short time. Press on my sisters, the journey must go on! But for those days in which you need to remember God's promises for you, here are a few:

- *"The LORD will fight for you; you need only to be still." –*Exodus 14:14 (NIV)

- *"He gives strength to the weary and increases the power of the weak."* –Isaiah 40:29 (NIV)

- *"So do not fear, for I am with you; do not be dismayed, for I am your God. I will strengthen you and help you; I will uphold you with My righteous right hand."* –Isaiah 41:10 (NIV)

- *"Though the mountains be shaken and the hills be removed, yet My unfailing love for you will not be shaken nor my covenant of peace be removed," says the LORD, who has compassion on you."* –Isaiah 54:10 (NIV)

- *"No weapon forged against you will prevail, and you will refute every tongue that accuses you. This is the heritage of the servants of the LORD, and this is their vindication from Me," declares the LORD.*—Isaiah 54:17 (NIV)

- *"The LORD Himself goes before you and will be with you; He will never leave you nor forsake you. Do not be afraid; do not be discouraged."* – Deuteronomy 31:8 (NIV)

- *For I know the plans I have for you…to prosper you and not to harm you, plans to give you hope and a future."* –Jeremiah 29:11 (NIV)

Questions for Reflection:

1. What negative feelings are you feeling in this season? What can you do to combat those feelings?

2. If you have gone back to your situation before, how did it end? Are you willing to go through it again?

3. Who are the people that will get you through your desert season? What can you learn from them?

4. What mistakes have you made in your desert season that may be prolonging it? How can you prevent yourself from making them again?

5. How can you use the Word of God to help you through your desert season?

6. What are the promises God has spoken over your life? What do you have to look forward to at the end of your desert season?

Notes:

Prayer

Heavenly Father,

My sister is going through a season of transition right now. I pray, that like the people of Israel in the desert, You will guide her through this desert season of her life. May You be a cloud that shades her and covers her in her moments of weakness, and a fire that illuminates the way in moments of darkness.

I pray that You reveal the areas that she still needs to work on so that she may begin to heal. I pray that You work in her life rapidly so that she may fulfill her purpose in Your perfect timing.

In Jesus name, Amen.

-Chapter Seven-

SHE WILL KNOT QUIT
PART 2 OF THE DESERT SEASON

"But one thing I do: Forgetting what is behind and
straining toward what is ahead"
—Philippians 3:13

Now as you continue to walk through your desert season, it would be wise to also use that time to prepare for your next season. If you were anything like me, your last season might have stripped you of your own identity. You might have felt like you lost sight of who you were in the midst of your pain. Right now is when you may have the most desire to quit, but I dare you to keep going. This is the time when looking forward to what's ahead of you matters most. The desert season is the perfect time to rebuild yourself so that when you arrive at your next season you will arrive whole and not broken.

STEP 5: GRIEVING

The first thing you need to do in order to rebuild yourself is to acknowledge your feelings. When we let go of something or when there is a loss, it is human nature to grieve. Ignoring your feelings will not make them go away. In order to start rebuilding, you will first need to grieve your loss.

In the book, *The Complete Guide to Crisis and Trauma Counseling,* Dr. H. Norman Wright states the following:

> Genuine grief is the deep sadness and weeping that expresses the acceptance of

our inability to do anything about our losses. It is a prelude to letting go, to relinquishment. It is dying that precedes resurrection" (Wright 86).

This statement resonated with me because it made me realize that I needed to grieve in order to be able to let go. I needed to accept that there was nothing more I could do about my loss and that it made me sad. If you don't let out the pain and deal with those feelings, letting go will become an impossible task and the desert will become a permanent home for you.

That being said, I want to normalize what you may be feeling as you grieve. When we look at a dictionary definition of grief some of the synonyms you will find to describe it are: sorrow, misery, sadness, anguish, pain, distress, heartbreak, agony, torment, affliction, suffering and despair. You know what these words make me think of? Hell; and grieving feels a lot like you're going through hell while everyone else seems to be fine. It is for this reason that the grieving process is often the loneliest.

Although each and every one of us at some point or another has or will experience grief, we each experience grief differently. Unfortunately, there are no steps I can provide you on how to do it properly, nor can I give you insight on how long your grief will last. Grief is much like a fingerprint, we all have it and experience it, but it is unique to the person experiencing it.

Given that we each may be feeling the same feelings when we grieve, it is the way we react to those feelings that will vary from person to person. Grief is something that you will have to work through. It is a process of its own that begins with us asking why and progresses as we begin to ask how (Wright 86). The why questions we ask are always about why the loss happened? When we begin to cope with the loss and accept it, those "why's" turn into "how's" where you begin to ask, "how can I learn from this experience?" (Wright 86).

However, before we can begin to learn from it, we must go through the process. One of the things that I did in my grieving process was to write a letter to the person I was letting go of. This was a letter that they would never get to read but it felt good to be able to get everything I was feeling out of my system and it really helped me to get past the "why" part of grieving and more into the "how" part. Something else you can do is find specific times and places in your day to designate for grieving, crying and letting out what you're feeling in private between you and God. Set a timer for yourself and when you're timer goes off, move on to the next part of your day (Wright 115). I find this to be a better option than holding in what you're feeling and exploding at the wrong moment. It is important that we allow ourselves to deal with what we are feeling in healthy ways and not just ignore it.

I remember when I first began grieving and hadn't found healthy ways to deal with it. I had a meltdown and it was very bad timing. In the previous chapter I mentioned that I thought my desert season had ended until something happened that made me realize that it hadn't. That "something" was grief. I had walked into a place that triggered thoughts about plans I had made, and now that I had let go, those plans would never come to pass. Grief isn't just about what or whom you lost in the past or present, it's also about the things you lost in the future because they never had the opportunity to happen. Sometimes those are the things that hurt the most. But it is those same things we need to grieve and cry over.

I urge you my sisters, just let it all out. Pretending that you are fine will only go so far before grief catches up with you. You went through a bad time in your life.

You have the right to feel sad, angry, and frustrated. That's why it is important to have people in your support network that will love you unconditionally and can be there for you in those moments when you cannot continue pretending that everything is fine.

You will experience pain and sorrow but as it says in Psalm 30:5, *"weeping may endure for a night, but rejoicing comes in the morning"* (NIV). What you sow in weeping will always be reaped in joy. I promise you this my sister, if you grieve now for the desires you had that will never come to pass, God will honor your tears and replace your sorrow with the joy of new desires, of new dreams, and of new opportunities. That too is His manna for you.

STEP 6: FORGIVING

Once you have begun your grieving process, you will need to begin to deal with another painful thing, having to forgive. I know that this is difficult when you have been hurt. You may even have the desire to stop reading now because when you're hurting, talking about forgiveness is like poking at a bad wound. But failing to forgive WILL hinder you from wholeness. Forgiveness, however, is a tricky thing. What makes forgiveness difficult sometimes is that the people who hurt us often don't apologize. Author Robert Brault stated, "Life becomes easier when you learn to accept an apology you never got". We often think that we need to *feel* like forgiving someone before we forgive them; and we really don't feel like forgiving until the person is sorry.

But in fact, forgiveness is a choice we must consciously make before we *feel* like forgiving. It's like expecting a car to run without turning it on. The choice to forgive is the key that must go into the ignition in order for the car to begin running. We must choose to forgive before we even feel we have forgiven. It has to be an intentional act.

Forgiveness is not a one day process. You may have to bring the person or people who hurt you to forgiveness many times. Every time you feel triggered to anger or resentment when you think of the person, you must bring them to forgiveness again. One of the things that helped me to forgive was when I began to look at the people who hurt me through a filter of empathy. Empathy enables you to step into someone else's shoes and see life from their perspective (this is what Jesus literally did for us). Empathy does not justify the person's actions but it does allow you to see beyond those actions in order to forgive.

When we look at someone who hurt us, all we see is what they did to us, but we fail to look at everything that has taken place in that person's life leading up to those actions. But we are a product of our experiences, and similar to grieving, the way we experience the things that happen in our lives and what we do with those experiences, differs from person to person.

For example, let's say that two children are raised in a home where the father was an alcoholic, and due to the alcohol he becomes abusive. One child may grow up and detest alcohol because of what he witnessed growing up, while the other may follow in his father's footsteps because that is how he learned to cope with life. They both experienced the same thing growing up, but had different outcomes in adulthood. We each internalize our experiences differently regardless of how similar they may be to someone else's experience.

Now let's say that the child who adopted drinking alcohol as a way to cope in his adulthood gets married and has children of his own. His drinking gets worse, he loses a job, he gets depressed, he drinks more. The wife is upset at her husband's lack of responsibility and eventually they lose their home and become homeless. The wife decides to leave with her children because she is unable to continue in the toxic situation. Who is to blame?

Do we blame the wife for getting involved with a man who had a drinking problem? Do we blame the husband for being an alcoholic? Do we blame the husband's parent? Do we blame the liquor store who sold him the alcohol? The government who makes this poison legal and accessible? If we do blame the husband's parent, do we bother to wonder what led him to become an alcoholic? The fact of the matter is that when we begin to play the blame game, no one wins.

We are all born clean slates. We are born innocent with no evil intent in us. But we are born into a fallen world and sooner or later as we begin to experience life we embrace our sinful nature and commit the atrocities that we do. The Word says that all are guilty of sin and have fallen short of God's glory (Romans 3:23). Someone has hurt you, but you have also hurt others in your life. At some level we have all been marked by the things we've gone through, and because of those things we don't always act the way that we should towards others. When we begin to understand that even the worst of us is a product of our experiences, it starts to get just a little easier to forgive and let go.

When I began to see the people who hurt me from the lens of empathy, I was able to begin praying for them. Now, listen to what I just said. I said praying FOR them, not ABOUT them. Complaining to God about what the person did to you or how hard it is to forgive them, will not help you to forgive, and you will only repeat to God what He already knows. You need to pray with the knowledge that your battle is not against flesh and blood (Ephesians 6:12).

The Bible goes on to tell us what our battle is against. It states that it is against *"principalities, against powers, against the rulers of the darkness of this age, against spiritual hosts of wickedness in the heavenly places"* (Ephesians 6:12). When we pray for those who harmed us, we pray that God will restore them. We pray with the knowledge that there are evil and demonic spiritual forces that entice and manipulate people.

We must pray that God will transform and heal their lives and that they will come to a knowledge of Christ so that they will not continue to cause harm unto others. Forgiveness does not make you the weaker person. It makes you the stronger person. The weakness is in running back to the same situation and repeatedly allowing yourself to get hurt. It is difficult to forgive when you are continuously being hurt by the same person over and over again. That is why I repeat once again, that boundaries are necessary. Without boundaries you will have an extremely difficult time forgiving because you need space away from the person or situation in order to let go of all the negative feelings you may feel towards them.

Forgiveness will help you come out of your desert season with a clean mind and heart. When we know what needs to be fixed in us, our prayers can become more specific and we can be more intentional in getting out of our desert season.

Another reason we need to forgive is so that we will be forgiven. When Jesus was teaching His disciples about praying to the Father, He stated the following: *"And when you stand praying, if you hold anything against anyone, forgive them, so that your Father in heaven may forgive you your sins"* (Mark 11:25). Jesus makes it plain and simple; if you don't forgive, you will not be forgiven. Not forgiving, when you have been forgiven by God, is a hypocritical act.

We do not deserve forgiveness. It was freely given to us by Jesus Christ, who chose to sacrifice His own life through a gruesome death in order to forgive us. If He could go through that to forgive us, then I believe we are capable of forgiving.

Now, I am not belittling the acts of other people toward us, but I will say that God is also a God of justice. The Word says the following in Romans 12:19, *"Do not take revenge, my dear friends, but leave room for God's wrath, for it is written: 'It is mine to avenge; I will repay', says the Lord"*(NIV). When someone does a wrong and does not repent, you just have to allow time to take its course and God will enact justice. Galatians 6:7 (NIV) states, *"Do not be deceived: God cannot be mocked. A man reaps what he sows"*. We may be fooled by people and may feel powerless to do anything about it but God cannot be mocked.

Do not misunderstand what I'm trying to say. I am not saying that you should pray for vengeance. But you should forgive and leave it in God's hands. Consequences are simply a way of reminding us to get back in line with what God expects of us.

'We can only reap the fruit of freedom when we have sown the seeds of forgiveness.

Nelson Mandela once stated that "resentment is like drinking poison and then hoping it will kill your enemies". I believe lack of forgiveness works in the same way. You won't do any harm to anyone but yourself when you refuse to forgive others. We can only reap the fruit of freedom when we have sown the seeds of forgiveness.

Forgiving Yourself

But forgiveness isn't just about others, sometimes you have to forgive yourself. At least I did. I can honestly say that I've always had an easy time forgiving myself for things I have done. I always thought, I'm human, I make mistakes, and it's time to get past this. But when I had to learn to let go in the solitude of my desert season and I really started to deal with the things inside me, I realized I hadn't forgiven myself for many things.

I hadn't forgiven myself for making the bad decisions I had made in the first place, and I hadn't forgiven myself for hurting people who were affected by my bad decisions. Now I don't know what your specific situation is, but I do know that often times we come out of our season of bondage with a lot of guilt. We have guilt for many reasons. Sometimes for decisions we made, or for allowing other people to treat us a certain way. We might feel guilty because we hurt people. Yet, in the midst of all that guilt we manage to hold it together. But the thing about guilt is that we can only tolerate so much of it until we snap. It's like a rubber band. The more weight over that rubber band the closer it comes to snapping.

Today my rubber band snapped. I was driving in my car this morning and I began to think about how my decisions in the past had affected my mom. I thought about how I had made her feel when I made certain decisions that impacted her. Years had now gone by since I made these decisions but as I thought about them, tears began to swell up in my eyes; they were tears of anger and resentment towards myself. I realized at that moment that I hadn't forgiven myself.

I went to counseling that evening and discussed with my counselor that I felt I hadn't forgiven myself. I began to cry again, not just tears, but deep heaving painful tears. My counselor asked me a question that kept me thinking for a while. She asked me, "What does it mean to forgive yourself?" What did it mean? I knew that I didn't want to feel as terrible as I did when I thought about my bad decisions. But I had never had to forgive myself for anything so serious. What I was feeling now was a sense of self-condemnation.

Condemnation is like this nagging voice in your subconscious that is constantly saying, "Remember what you did! Remember what you did!" In order to forgive yourself you must silence that voice. You must send it away. **The first step is to recognize that this voice does not come from God** because in fact God is saying the opposite to you.

In Jeremiah 31:34 God states, *"For I will forgive their iniquity, and their sin I will <u>remember no more</u>."* The same statement is reaffirmed in the New Testament in Hebrews 8:12. Anytime I see something written in both the Old and New Testament of the Bible, I make it a point to remember it. Repetition is a writer's way of getting the reader to remember something (on a side note, what have I repeated so far? Something to think about). Going back to this Scripture, I want you to replace "their" with your name. For me it would be, "For I will forgive Sasha's iniquity and her sin I will remember no more". Isn't that powerful? Condemnation says "remember" but the voice of God says, "remember no more".

Condemnation says "remember" but the voice of God says, "remember no more".

The second step is to replace that deceitful voice of condemnation with the truth of God's voice. Philippians 4:8 reminds us, *"Finally brothers, whatever is true, whatever is noble, whatever is right, whatever is pure, whatever is lovely, whatever Is admirable...think about these things".* All of these attributes describe God. We must think about what God has to say about us because all that He says is true. Conversely, the voice of condemnation is the dark voice of the enemy and it is filled with lies. If we don't silence that accusing voice and replace it with God's voice, we run the risk of giving into the condemnation and allowing it to become our reality. If you don't confront it, you will conform to it. We must cast down any thought that lifts itself against God's truth or knowledge (2 Corinthians 10:5)

The third step is to let go of the memory of the past that you are torturing yourself with and replace it with positive memories of the present. Instead of focusing all your attention and energy on what you did wrong in the past, focus it on what you are doing or can do correctly now. The Apostle Paul gives us some words of experience in Philippians 3:13. He says, *"But one thing I do: Forgetting what is behind and straining toward what is ahead."* Continue to focus on what is ahead of you. You made a mistake in the past, but moving forward, make it a point not to repeat that mistake again.

The last step is to verbally forgive yourself. Say it out loud. The Bible tells us that God declares the things that aren't as if they were (Romans 4:17). As His children we have the authority to do the same by speaking by faith. Don't wait until you feel you have forgiven yourself, just begin to declare it over yourself. Your own declarations will break you free of condemnation.

When I finally spoke the words, "I forgive myself", I believe something changed inside of me. A stronghold and pattern of thought that told me I could not forgive myself, was broken. I gave life to myself again and broke open the jail cell of condemnation that had me knotted up inside. The thing is that God already forgave you. Why should you continue to condemn yourself when the Bible says that *"there is now no condemnation for those who are in Christ"* (Romans 8:1)? You are a new creation in Him. Whatever you did in the past has been erased from His book. He has set you free, so be free from your own self-judgment.

Forgiving God

However, there is a third factor I must add when we discuss forgiveness, and that is forgiving God. Now this is an interesting concept because in reality God doesn't need to be forgiven as He is God and does no wrong. But I find that many times when we are letting go and we were not ready to do so, we grow angry and resentful towards God and we often blame Him for our misery. We ask things like, "Why did you allow this to happen?" or "If you are God why didn't you fix this?" In those moments we run the risk of becoming like the criminal hanging on the cross next to Jesus on the day He was crucified.

But in fact there were two men hanging on the cross with Jesus. Both were criminals.

> *"One of the criminals who hung there hurled insults at Him: 'Aren't you the Messiah? Save yourself and us!' But the other criminal rebuked him, 'Don't you fear God', he said, 'since you are under the same sentence? We are punished justly for our deeds, for we are getting what our deeds deserve but this man has done nothing wrong'. Then He said, 'Jesus remember me when you come into your kingdom.' Jesus*

answered him, 'Truly I tell you, today you will be with me in paradise'" (Luke 23:39-43).

These men were both being punished for their crimes. They were both about to die. Jesus was the only one who could truly save their lives. He, after all, was the Savior. One man is humble and recognizes his wrong doings. He doesn't even ask Jesus for anything more than to have a place in His memories. The other man in his pride insults and blames Jesus for not getting him off the cross. Jesus doesn't respond to the man who insults Him. But He ensures the eternal well-being of the man who approached Him in humility. My point is that since God is really the only one who can help you get through this process, blaming Him and being angry at Him, is probably not the wisest thing to do. In other words, don't bite the hand that feeds you.

When we come to God with accusations and with blame for what we are going through, those feelings come from a place of pride whether we want to admit it or not. The moment that we begin to blame and accuse God we have chosen to sit on the throne of judgment and have elevated our position above God's.

When things that are unfair happen to us it is a natural response to be angry. Sometimes, we become angry at the person who hurt us, sometimes we become angry with ourselves and sometimes when we find nowhere else to place blame, we get angry at God. But in order to get past this we need to explore some things about God. We are taught that God is good and all powerful, that is why when bad things happen to us we enter into a conflict with God. But it is because God is good that bad things happen to us (but before you accuse me of being anti-Biblical, keep reading). You see, there are two characteristics of God that we often forget about when we are going through difficult situations in our lives. One is that God is all knowing and the other is that God is love.

Let's begin with the fact that God is all-knowing. There are various Scriptures in the Bible that point to this fact. 1 John 3:20 (NIV) states, *"If our hearts condemn us, we know that God is greater than our hearts, and He knows everything"*. Psalm 147:5 (NIV) states, *"Great is our Lord and mighty in power; His understanding has no limit"*. In Isaiah 55:8-9 (NIV) God is quoted saying, *"For My thoughts are not your thoughts neither are your ways My ways...as the heavens are higher than the earth, so are My ways higher than your ways and My thoughts higher than your thoughts*". In Isaiah 46:10 (NIV) God is also quoted saying, "*I make known the end from the beginning, from ancient times, what is still to come...*"

All of these Scriptures point to one idea and that is that God knows all things. He knows our hearts, His understanding has no limit, His way of thinking is on a higher level than ours and He sees the big picture because He knows what will happen in the end from the beginning. This means that when things happen in our lives that are outside of our understanding and that sometimes cause us pain, there is a whole bigger picture that we are not seeing. God has the full picture.

As I was going through this whole process, even before I had to let go, I would question God all the time. I would ask Him, "why can't you just fix this?" "Why can't you make the pain go away?" "Why can't you stop this person from hurting me?" While I was in the situation I couldn't see the bigger picture of my life. I could only see what I was going through at that moment. If God had done any of the things I had asked Him to do in that season of my life, I may have been in a worse situation right now. In retrospect, I am happy that God did not answer my prayers at that time because I am happier now than I ever would have been had I stayed in that situation.

But God knew that then. He knew I would be happier out of the situation than I would have been if He would have answered my prayers and I would have continued in it. He knew that in allowing me to feel the pain and go through the misery I went through, I would get out of that place sooner. I would be happier sooner. Not only would I be happier sooner, but I would begin writing this book sooner. You would read it sooner. It would all happen in His perfect timing because He knows what will happen in the end from the beginning. So yes, sometimes God does allow things to happen because He sees the full picture and knows what will be best for you in the long run.

This brings me to the second characteristic about God I would like to address, the fact that He is a loving God. I need you to piece this together in order to understand the full concept. When the all-knowing God, who knows the end from the beginning, created man, He did so with the knowledge that man would sin. That knowledge included the fact that the only way man would still be able to continue his relationship with God after sinning would be through the death of God's only son, Jesus Christ.

My question is why would God do that? Why even create man if He knew from the beginning this would be the result? John 3:16 goes on to tell us that the reason God sent His son into the world and allowed Him to be sacrificed was because He loved us and wanted to save us from perishing. God is a God of love. Love is not just what He does, it is who He is, so all of His actions are a result of who He is. If His reason for saving humanity from death was that He loved it, then this must also mean creating humanity in the first place was also done out of love.

So, God creates the first man and woman, and because He acts out of love He gives them a gift, free will. Why? Because love without free will is not love, it is obligation. God created us with free will so that we have the option to choose to love Him. On the down side, free will also meant we could choose not to love Him. We could choose not to obey Him, not to follow Him; we can even choose not to believe in Him. That is where man fails. Adam and Eve make the choice not to love, obey, follow, or believe in God. They choose to believe the serpent in the garden who lies to them. In choosing in this manner, they break off the relationship with God and it is God who takes the initiative to restore it once again by sending His son to die on the cross many years later.

As detrimental as free will can be, God does not take it away from humanity. There are people who will use free will to hurt others. God will not override our will to stop us from making bad decisions because He is a King and once He declares something He cannot take it back. He gave us free will, and He will not take it away. It is possible that someone may have used their free will to hurt you. Just as it is possible that you have made decisions that have lead you to be in the predicament you are in now. If either of those are the case, God cannot be blamed for humanity's wrongful use of its free will.

If you desire to live, to love, and to be free, then free will is necessary, and a loving God gave it to us. Our distortion of the intention for which God gave us free will is not His fault. To think that would be the equivalent of blaming someone who designed a knife to cut fruit, for someone else's misuse of the knife kill. God's motives are always pure. At best, He is looking at the bigger picture of your life that you cannot see, and at worst, our pain is a product of the misuse of a good gift that He gave us.

Diseases, natural disasters and everything else that is outside of human control is still the result of a fallen and broken world suffering the consequences of free will being misused. The Bible states in Romans 8:20-22 that all of creation itself is in bondage because of corruption. Humanity is the source of that corruption.

As I previously stated, anger and frustration are natural responses in the process of letting go, but God truly loves you and has your best interest at heart. Take the blame off of Him, pull your anger away from Him and ask Him to forgive you for the resentment you've held towards Him. His desire is to help you through this process. If reconciliation between you and Him is needed, now would be the time to do so.

STEP 7: REBUILDING

One of the things I did when I was in my desert season was that I began to rebuild myself in all areas. I had come out of my Egypt, broken and with low self-esteem. I had no real sense of self-worth and could barely recognize myself. I claimed I did, but that past season had broken me in ways I hadn't even realized. Now it was time to rebuild myself.

Your own declarations will break you free of condemnation.

Physically, I decided I would start eating healthier. My body needed to be detoxified from the years of emotional eating I had done. Before I had finally decided to let go, I had let myself go. I can't remember how many days I felt so depressed that all I wanted to do was drown my sorrows in chocolate ice cream or chocolate chip cookies and hot chocolate (I had a thing with chocolate. Who am I kidding, I still do). Anyway, during that time I had gained about forty pounds and every new pound pushed me further and further into a place of dissatisfaction and depression.

When I was in my desert season I realized that my eating was tied to my emotions. I began to read a book by Lysa Terkeurst titled, "Made to Crave", and it was definitely a life-changer for me in this season. It made me realize that I was turning to food to deal with my issues instead of turning to God. I began to look at food differently and I actually began to enjoy healthy eating. Every day I'd come home and look up healthy recipes online and I was actually motivated to cook. I began to lose weight just by changing my eating habits. Even though I am not where I want to be yet, I'm not where I was before. I see progress!

However, that book by Lysa Terkeurst was only one of the many I began to read in my desert season. I suddenly had a craving for reading. Reading was my new escape. It was my place to go to in order to replace my negative thoughts with positive ones. I began to read inspirational books, books about healing, books about self-care, and even some books that were just for fun (I've added a list of book suggestions at the end of this book). Although reading isn't for everyone, I encourage you to find a way to begin to fill your mind with positive words, whether it be reading, listening to sermons, or positive music It is so crucial to replace negative thinking with positive thinking in this season.

I also began going to counseling. Counseling really helped me to refocus my attention on rebuilding myself and it helped me understand why I had made the decisions I had previously made and how to avoid making them again. Many times there are patterns in our lives that lead us to make the same types of bad decisions over and over again, and if we don't break free of these patterns of thinking, we will continue to live a life of bondage. Contrary to what some may think, counseling is not for crazy people, it's for all people who have ever gone through something difficult, including having to let go.

Going to counseling helped me in rebuilding myself, but my counselor was also a vital part of my support network. Earlier we discussed the importance of having a support network and the kind of people you might want to have in that group. At this point in your letting go process, your support network will also be vital in helping you to rebuild yourself.

I had started visiting a new church as well in which I felt accepted and in which I was helped with my healing process. This was one of those changes of scenery I had to do in order to set some boundaries in my life. I also needed people who I knew would able to encourage me and walk me through the process of letting go. The church I found (which I'm still attending) was able to do this for me and that helped me when it came to rebuilding myself spiritually.

STEP 8: REDISCOVERING

After I began to rebuild myself, I realized I had to rediscover myself. I wasn't the same person who had started this journey. My experience had changed me and I couldn't go back to being who I was before I went through my situation. There was another question to be answered. Who am I now?

I was so accustomed to being around someone else that being alone was foreign to me. I had to rediscover who I was when I was on my own. It was in my rediscovery that I realized I loved books. I also learned that I have a pretty good sense of humor when I'm not walking around depressed and moping about life. I discovered I wanted to go back to school. I realized I wanted to help other women. I went back to writing. I spent time with friends. I was actually productive. But all of that happened because I took time to rediscover who I was now and I didn't get stuck in who I left behind.

The Sasha I had left behind was always sad. She was always tired, she didn't socialize much, she cried every day and her life was empty even though she was always surrounded by people. I think that there is nothing more exhilarating than really getting to know who you are. I found that for a good chunk of the time that I was stuck in my situation, I was being someone that others wanted me to be but I wasn't myself. I had lost part of my identity, and you most likely have too.

Now is the perfect time to rediscover yourself. You might find that things you didn't enjoy before, you do find pleasure in now and vice versa. I remember having a conversation with my cousin shortly after letting go of my situation. My cousin is a funny guy. He says many things, lots of which sound silly or obnoxious, but underneath all of that, there's usually some shred of wisdom in his comments.

He said to me, "you have to figure out who you are now. Maybe you want to go out and try something crazy". I said, "No I'm definitely not going to do anything crazy". He responded, "Okay so there you go, at least now you know you're not a crazy girl". I laughed at the moment but there was a shred of truth in what he was saying. I knew who I wasn't and that would make it easier to figure out who I was.

After you've healed, you have to figure out who you are now. What do you like? What don't you like? What kind of person have you become after rebuilding yourself? You must re-experience life from a new perspective. The beautiful part about rebuilding yourself is not that you change who are, but that you grow into the person God intended for you to be.

Maybe you can take yourself out on a date, and start getting to know the new you. You might be surprised at what you find. E.E. Cummings stated, "It takes courage to grow up and become who you really are". Let this be a time of courage in your life. Let this be a growing experience. Let this be the time that you are brave enough to be you without caring what people might have to say. But be comfortable in your own skin knowing that you are unique, that you are beautiful, that you are loved and that God has placed in your hands all the tools necessary to conquer your world.

Your desert season is beginning to come to an end and the wonderful thing about endings is that they are always followed by beginnings. This is your time! Make the best of it and enjoy the journey of getting to know the upgraded version of you. You are fierce darling, it's about time you embrace that inner queen.

Questions for Reflection:

1. Who are the people you feel you need to forgive?

2. Is there anything you need to forgive yourself for?

3. What can you do to begin rebuilding yourself?

4. Who are some positive people you can surround yourself with in this season?

5. What can you do to rediscover yourself?

Notes:

_____

_____

_____

_____

_____

_____

_____

_____

_____

_____

_____

_____

_____

_____

_____

_____

_____

_____

_____

_____

_____

Prayer

Father,

My prayer is that You help my sister to rebuild herself during her desert season. Help her to heal as she forgives others and herself. Give her the strength to keep pressing forward and focus on Your truth. Give her the wisdom to replace the voice of condemnation with Your voice of truth.

I ask that You bring positive people into her life. I pray for divine connections in her network of support. And most of all, help her to feel that You are near in this difficult time. Thank You because I know You are working in my sister's heart even as we speak.

In the name of Jesus, Amen.

-Chapter Eight-

SHE WILL KNOT HERSELF WITH CHRIST

"Take My yoke upon you...for My yoke is easy and My burden is light."—Matthew 11:29-30

STEP 9: STARTING OVER

When you begin to approach the end of your desert season, there are a few things that will happen. One, is that you will begin to regain confidence in who God called you to be. Two, is that you will be getting closer to the arrival of your next season and three, is that you will have begun to heal in many areas of your life. All of these are beautiful and wonderful things to experience and feel.

However, because of our going above and beyond tendencies, we must be careful not to make the same mistakes in the new season that we made in the past season. In order to prevent this from happening, you will have to take some preventative measures. Because you now recognize your own value, you will have to tie yourself up again so as to avoid being tied up by another situation or person. But this time, you will tie or knot yourself with Christ.

Have you ever heard the expression "tying the knot"? Usually you hear this phrase in reference to two people getting married. When a couple decides to get married it is said that they have decided to "tie the knot". The term refers to hand fasting ceremonies which were part of marriage rituals in the past. These ceremonies were symbolic of two people being united as one through marriage. When Rebekah arrived in Canaan the first thing that happened was that she and Isaac "tied the knot" or got married. Let me pause right here before we get ahead of ourselves. Arriving to your "promised land" is not the equivalent of getting married. Especially if you are letting go of a relationship. For Rebekah, her promise was her marriage but that's not what we're about to discuss here.

Like Rebekah with Isaac, the first thing that should happen when you exit your desert season is that you enter into a deep commitment with Jesus Christ and "tie the knot" with Him. This might come easily to you because through your desert season you had to hold on to God in order to overcome many obstacles. However, for many, once they arrive at the "Promised Land" like the people of Israel did, it becomes easy to forget what God has done for you. What you will have to do now, is to tie yourself or yoke yourself with Christ. The Bible makes reference to this in Matthew 11:28-30:

> *Come to Me, all you who labor and are heavy laden, and I will give you rest. Take My yoke upon you and learn from Me, for I am gentle and lowly in heart, and you will find rest for your*

souls. For My yoke is easy and My burden is light.

Verse 28 states that all those who labor and are burdened should come to Christ. Some of us have already taken this step at this point (if you haven't, the last chapter of the book shows you how to do so). Earlier we discussed Psalm 55:22 which stated that we should cast our burdens on the Lord and He will sustain us. When we bring these verses together with Matthew 11:29 which states that we should take God's yoke upon us, we are able to gain a broader understanding of what God is trying to tell us.

But before I explain that, let me explain what a yoke is. According to Merriam Webster dictionary, a yoke is "a wooden bar or frame by which two draft animals (such as oxen) are joined at the heads or necks for working together". When the Bible states that we are to cast our burdens on the Lord and He will sustain us, I believe it is referencing the fact that Christ will yoke Himself with you in order to carry your burdens so that you will not have to carry them alone. Thinking of this actually makes me think back to when Jesus was forced to carry the burden of the cross all the way up to Golgotha. It is there that He threw our yoke upon Himself by carrying that wooden frame called the cross.

But it doesn't end there, verse 29 says that we are to put on His yoke so that we can learn from Him. When two animals are yoked together in order to work, usually a more experienced animal is placed with a less experienced animal so that the less experienced animal can learn from the experienced one. Christ asks us to yoke ourselves with Him, not only so that He can help us carry our burdens, but so that we can learn how to deal with the burdens of life and so that He can instruct us in the correct ways.

He then states that when we do this we will find rest for our souls because His yoke is easy and His burden is light, meaning that the work He requires us to do is not meant to burden us. Remember when we discussed earlier in the book how we take on burdens that God hasn't asked us to take on? Well the only burden God asks us to take on is the one He assigns us, and that burden should not exhaust us. Instead when we carry that burden with Him, we will still feel well-rested. Contrary to our "over-achiever" mentalities will have us believe, God actually wants us to rest. This is so true that it is actually one of our Ten Commandments. You've gone through a lot in this process, God wants you to learn to rest too. Don't underestimate the power of rest as you enter your new season.

In order to prosper in your new season, you must yoke yourself to Christ and let Him guide you through that new season. Without Him you will walk into your new season aimlessly, and will very likely take burdens upon yourself again that weren't meant for you.

So, how can we yoke ourselves with Christ? We do this by having consistent intimacy with Him. I am sure that when Rebekah married Isaac she must have had to spend a lot of time with him in order to really get to know him. In the same way, we must spend time in intimacy with God in order to know Him and His thoughts and plans for our lives. The Bible states in Psalm 51:6 that God desires truth in the innermost being and that in the hidden parts He will make known wisdom to us. I believe these hidden parts the Bible refers to are our intimate moments with God in prayer and meditation. Prayer is simply talking to God. You don't have to have a degree in theology to do it. Just talk to Him as you would talk with a close friend.

Aside from this, the Bible also states in Psalm 119:105 that God's word is a *"lamp to our feet and a light to our path"*. The more time you spend delving into the Word of God and studying who God is, the more God will reveal and illuminate the path you should take. Any relationship requires time and communication. Your relationship with God is no exception. You must put time into the relationship.

Don't wait until you find some free time. Be intentional. Set your alarm. Wake up half an hour earlier every day. Spend a little of that time in prayer and then read Scripture and meditate on what God is trying to say to you through His Word. Starting your day in the presence of God will set a great foundation for your relationship. Doing so will help you to seek out the purpose that God has for your life. Only then will you find satisfaction for your life and only then will you prevent yourself from falling into the same traps you fell into in the past. So put on that yoke and get to work with Christ on the life He's called you to.

Questions for Reflection:

1. What can you do to deepen your relationship with God in this new season?

2. Are there burdens or habits that you have carried into this new season that God hasn't asked you to carry? How can you get rid of them?

3. Are there things about God you desire to know? If so, what are they and how can you go about learning them?

Notes:

_____

_____

_____

_____

_____

_____

_____

_____

_____

_____

_____

_____

_____

_____

_____

_____

_____

_____

_____

Prayer

Lord Jesus,

I pray that my sister will enter into a deeper relationship with You as she exits her desert season. May she tie herself to You like never before so that Your spirit may guide her and direct her. I declare that she will not fall into the same traps of the past.

May Your word be the guiding light that helps her make wise decisions and leads her to the bright future You have prepared for her.

I pray that any residue from her past will be removed right now so that she may live a life free from her past mistakes.

In Jesus name, Amen.

-Chapter Nine-

SHE WILL KNOT FORGET

"And they overcame him by the blood of the Lamb
and by the word of their testimony..."
—Revelation 12:11

STEP 10: HELPING OTHERS

In the beginning of this book, when I was telling Rebekah's story, I stated that her descendants were part of the lineage that lead to the birth of Jesus Christ. I then asked, what would have happened if Rebekah didn't let go of her family? What would have happened if she would have remained in Mesopotamia in the city of Nahor? She wouldn't have been part of this greater purpose that would bring about the Savior of humanity into the world.

I'd like to remind you that Rebekah had a say in all this. She had a choice. When Abraham's servant asked Abraham what he should do if the woman he found didn't want to return back to Canaan with him, Abraham's response was that he would be released from his oath. This means that Rebekah could have chosen not to go with him. Again, when Rebekah was given the choice of staying an extra ten days with her family or going with Abraham's servant, the choice was up to her. In the same way, you have a choice.

You can choose to walk back into the same traps of being tied up and burdened in things that God never asked you to take on, or you can take on the greater plan and calling that God has for your life. Rebekah was brave enough to step into the unknown and fulfill

God's purpose without even knowing how great the outcome would be.

But Rebekah's decision to do so, had immediate effects. The Bible states that when Rebekah married Isaac, he was comforted after the death of his mother. Rebekah had just let go of her family and traveled through a season in the desert. When she arrived she found herself with an Isaac who still needed to let go of his mother after her death. Rebekah went from being the one who needed to be comforted in the desert by others, to being the comforter in someone else's desert season. Part of Rebekah's purpose at that moment in time was to comfort Isaac. Had she waited longer, or decided not to come at all, Isaac would not have been comforted after the death of his mother.

When God has brought you out of your desert season and into a new season, part of your role in God's greater purpose will be to help restore and comfort others who are still going through their desert season. The Apostle Paul reiterates this in 2 Corinthians 1:3-4 (NIV) when he states, *"Praise be to the God and Father of our Lord Jesus Christ, the Father of compassion and the God of all comfort, who comforts us in all our troubles, so that we can comfort those in any trouble with the comfort we ourselves receive from*

God". After God has restored and comforted you, He will use you to carry out His work of comforting and restoring others in their time of need. This will be part of the yoke you will carry with Christ.

Now, let me clarify something, I am not implying that God makes you go through bad situations in order to help others. What I am saying is that even when we make bad decisions that put us into bad situations, God finds ways to make beauty out of our ashes (Isaiah 61:3). He produces purpose and light for others out of our mistakes and pain so that our pain will not be in vain. Not only will He restore you, but He will restore others through you.

The Bible states that we will overcome by the blood of the lamb and the word of our testimony (Revelation 12:11). This is a powerful Scripture because it displays how God works to defeat the enemy. His blood which represents His sacrifice that brought about salvation and healing does the final work, but it is our testimony of how God has healed and delivered us that will draw the common ground between us and those who are broken and in need of deliverance.

Your pain is part of your testimony. It is nothing to be ashamed of, especially when God has delivered you from a bad situation. It is reason to glorify God and to

"...Even when we make bad decisions that put us into bad situations, God finds ways to make beauty out of our ashes ."

share what He has done for you. Just as people walked into your life in your desert season to help you, you will walk into others' lives at an appointed time to help them. God will guide you to them and you will help them through their desert season as well.

This book is the tool that God has given me to help other women going through the process of letting go. I chose to write it as I went through the process of letting go, because I wanted you as a reader to feel like I was right there with you in your desert season. I may not be with you in person but I pray that the Spirit of the Living God will transcend through this book and comfort you and empower you in your time of need so that you may do the same for others.

There are other women waiting on you. There are Isaac's and Rebekah's going through their desert season and struggling to let go and they are waiting on you to walk into their lives at a precise moment.

One of the things that helped me stick to my decision of letting go was that I held myself accountable for you and for anyone else reading this book who was in need of letting go. I understood that God wanted to make use of my experience in order to help other women overcome as well. When you understand the power of the purpose that God has deposited in you, you will not look back in desire of going back. You will only look back and see those who follow in your footsteps on the path to freedom and a purpose-filled life.

Because of them, you will not do the bare minimum, you will not be delayed, you will not cling to the familiar, you will not give up, you will knot yourself with Christ, and you will not forget the purpose for which you have been called. The Spirit of the Living God is within you, and He will be with you always as you continue on this journey through life.

Questions for Reflection:

1. What would have happened to you if you didn't let go?

2. Who are the people that God is putting in your path that are going through what you have already gone through?

3. How can you reach out to them and/or help them?

4. What is your testimony?

5. What tool will you use to help others struggling with letting go?

Notes:

_____

_____

_____

_____

_____

_____

_____

_____

_____

_____

_____

_____

_____

_____

_____

_____

_____

_____

_____

_____

_____

_____

_____

_____

Prayer

Father,

I pray that just as Rebekah was able to fulfill the purpose for which You called her, that my sister will be able to do the same. I pray that she use this second chance as an opportunity to help other women who have had trouble letting go.

Guide her in Your ways so that she may always be found immersed in You. May she be a comforter to those in need of comforting, a light to those in darkness, and a voice of hope to those in desperation. And may she forever be grateful for all You have done for her.

In Jesus name, Amen.

-Chapter Ten-

SHE WILL KNOT BE ASHAMED

"I sought the Lord, and He answered me; He delivered me from all my fears. Those who look to Him are radiant; their faces are never covered with shame"
—Psalm 34:4-5 (NIV)

As we reach the end of this book, I feel as though there is a confession I have to make. As I was writing this book I was battling with myself about whether or not I should discuss what it was I needed to let go of. I wanted to be transparent with you as the reader but I also wanted to protect the parties involved; and partially, I wanted to protect myself from being judged. I was, in a sense, afraid to tell what happened. But after realizing that I've asked you, the reader, to share your testimony with others, it seems only right that I be transparent in sharing my testimony with you.

After reading Psalm 34:4-5 which states that those who look to God will never be ashamed, I came to the conclusion that God knows my heart and the intention behind this book, and that He will not let me be shamed by it. So I will not be ashamed. By this point, I think that we've established enough common ground between us that I can tell you my story. So here it goes.

When I was twenty-three years old (2014), I had what might have been the best year of my life. That year I graduated from college with my bachelor's degree, I obtained my driver's license (I know it took me forever, don't judge me) and I published my first book titled, "With Purpose on Purpose". The last big thing I did that year was get married. Getting married was the decision that caused the downward spiral of events that lead to the writing of this book.

Before I got married I had three different dreams that were very similar in nature. The three dreams were warnings of what would happen if I continued in the relationship with the person I was planning to marry. I disregarded the dreams. Before I had even begun dating the person I married, my mother said to me, "Sasha, I know you guys are getting close but be careful, that man is not what God has planned for you". I disregarded my mother. I had been in and out of a relationship with this individual for about two years before we got married. The last time we had broken up, my pastor at the time said to me, "Sasha, I know you love him, but I think maybe it's best if you two just go your separate ways". I disregarded my pastor.

On September 22nd, 2014 I tied the knot. We got married in secret and no one from my family was present. There's a Spanish saying that says, "Lo que comienza mal, termina mal". It means that what doesn't begin well, will not end well. Needless to say, things did not end well between us. I'm not going to go into detail over what happened because I don't feel it's necessary.

I will say that three years into the marriage I was filing for divorce. I had every Biblically acceptable reason for doing so. I will also say that the issues in the marriage that arose began before we even hit the one year mark. We were going to church and sought advice from the pastors of the church we were attending. We also went to marriage counseling. I tell you this because I want you to understand that when I decided to file for divorce it was not a rash or hasty decision. I don't want anyone who reads this book to think that I am advocating for divorce because I fully believe in the sanctity of marriage and the fact that it was established by God.

The decision was a difficult but well thought out one. I had tried everything I could possibly think of to try to save the marriage, but in the end I saw that no matter what I did, nothing was changing, except for me. I was changing. I was becoming a person I didn't recognize. I was depressed, I was angry, I was filled with resentment, and there were times where I had even contemplated suicide. I made the decision that I felt was necessary considering the extreme state of my situation.

I will say with no shame that I loved my ex-husband. When I left, it was not because of lack of love for him, but because I realized I needed to love myself, and if I continued in that toxic relationship I was going to lose my sanity and possibly my life.

It is by the grace and mercy of God that I am here, alive and free to tell you how God brought a message out of my mess. The message is this: You are a daughter of God, and as such it is not only your right but your responsibility to be free from whatever is binding you and separating you from God and from the plan that God has for your life. You are part of God's great purpose. You have an identity, you are not worthless, and you are more valuable than the most precious rubies and stones the world can offer.

More importantly, you are loved by the Creator of the whole Universe. He loves you because He created you, and even now He will not abandon you in your mess. If He delivered me out of His mercy and love for me even when I disobeyed Him and didn't listen to the people He sent to warn me, then surely He will deliver you. You will never be too far gone to the point where He cannot reach you.

With that being said, I cannot close out this book without extending you an invitation to enter into a relationship with this God that I can't stop raving about, the God who helped me through this whole process. Maybe you know Him already, maybe you knew Him but have felt distant from Him for a long time, and maybe you've only heard of Him. Whatever the case may be, I can't finish this book without getting the opportunity to reintroduce Him to you.

The Bible says that God loved you so much that He gave His only Son so that He could take your place and die to pay the debt of your sin all so that you could have an eternal life (John 3:16). That eternal life begins now and never ends, and I believe God wants you to begin enjoying that eternal life with Him from this point on. So if you want to get to know this God who rescued me and who will happily do the same for you, then I ask you to repeat this prayer with me.

Father,

I thank You for giving up Your Son Jesus, to die for me. I repent of all my wrongdoings and I ask You to forgive me of my sins. I believe that Jesus died for me and resurrected so that I could have eternal life and enter into a relationship with You. Today I confess out loud that I accept You as my Lord and Savior and that I believe in You Jesus. Thank You for loving me. Thank You because I know I have now entered into a relationship with You. Thank You because You will never leave me and I will never have to feel alone again. In Jesus name, amen.

It's that simple. Having said this prayer doesn't mean that tomorrow you will stop sinning or that you will never fail God again. But it does mean that if and when you do, God will be right there to forgive you and pick you back up again so that you can keep walking with Him. So with that I leave you, and I congratulate you because today is the first day of the rest of your life. Thank you for taking this journey with me. May the Lord's goodness and mercy follow you everywhere that you go. I leave you with this Scripture as you press forward, may it be a constant word of encouragement in your heart and a guiding light in difficult times:

*"God is within her, **she will not** fall; [for] God will help her at break of day."*—Psalm 46:5 (NIV)

WORDS OF WISDOM FROM THOSE WHO HAVE WALKED THIS PATH BEFORE YOU...

As I've mentioned a few times throughout this book, at one point in my writing process I decided to send out a survey to women I was connected to on social media. I received about sixty responses to my survey which helped me shape and mold the direction of this book in some ways. To those of you who answered my survey, I want to say thank you. You are a vital resource to the writing of this book.

I'd like to share some of the advice that women who have already gone through the process of letting go were able to share. Two of the open-ended questions I asked in the survey were, what lessons these women learned when letting go, and what advice they would have given to their past selves about letting go. I will share the most common themes from their answers. I hope you will treasure these pearls of wisdom from some women who have walked in your shoes and overcome.

1. Don't be afraid of making tough decisions.
2. We cannot change those who do not wish to change for themselves.
3. God is with you every step of the way. Life goes on.

4. Keep moving forward. Stay positive.
5. Yes it's going to hurt but you will be okay in the end.
6. You need to think about what makes you happy too.
7. Measure people by their actions because actions speak louder than words.
8. Know your self-worth. Don't let anyone destroy your self-worth. You are better than this.
9. Don't doubt or second guess yourself.
10. Surround yourself with positive people that can support you.
11. Breathe, pray and walk away.
12. Focus on positive things ahead of you instead of on what you let go of.
13. Learn to listen to and trust God's voice and warnings.
14. God loves you and doesn't want you to hurt.
15. You use less strength by letting go.
16. There's a plan. You just can't see it yet.
17. You grow and you become stronger once you get through it.
18. Identify standards for the people you let into your life instead of settling for the bare minimum.
19. To better yourself you have to start with yourself.
20. The unknown can be scary but God's got you.

BOOKS TO READ WHILE LETTING GO

I'd also like to share a list of books that may be helpful during your letting go process. They really helped me, and if you're a reader I believe they will also help you.

1. *The Secret Things of God*
   By: Dr. Henry Cloud
2. *Boundaries*
   By: Dr. Henry Cloud
3. *Things I Wish I'd Known Before We Got Married*
   By: Gary Chapman
4. *The Five Love Languages*
   By: Gary Chapman
5. *Made to Crave*
   By: Lysa Terkeurst
6. *She's Still There*
   By: Chrystal Evans Hurst
7. *Fervent*
   By: Priscilla Shirer
8. *The Battlefield of the Mind*
   By: Joyce Meyer
9. *Jesus, The Man Who Loved Women,*
   By: Bruce Marchiano
10. *Finding God in My Loneliness*
    By: Lydia Brownback

Works Cited

"Home." *Lifeline*, Federal Substance Abuse and Mental Health Services Administration, suicidepreventionlifeline.org/.

Russell, Chris. "How to Make Right Decisions - Chris Russell." *Bible Study Tools*, Salem Web Network, www.biblestudytools.com/blogs/chris-russell/how-to-make-right-decisions.html.

Robinson, M.A., Blaine. "Marriage in Ancient Israel." *Marriage in Ancient Israel ~ Blaine Robison, M.A.*, 16 July 2012, www.blainerobison.com/hebroots/marriage-israel.htm.

Sarah Buel. "50 Obstacles to Leaving: 1-10." *The National Domestic Violence Hotline*, 18 Feb. 2018,www.thehotline.org/2013/06/10/50-obstacles-to-leaving-1-10/.

"Warning Signs." *Break the Cycle*, Let's Be Real, 6 Mar. 2018, www.breakthecycle.org/warning-signs?gclid=Cj0KCQjwyYHaBRDvARIsAHkAXcuY CgCrZYxZVXjZQ_rp99M-etS41KXPCs0whETAKJ2Jv-tA-R9WPXwaAg5HEALw_wcB

Wright, H. Norman. *The Complete Guide to Crisis & Trauma Counseling: What to Do and Say When It Matters Most!* Bethany House, 2014.

About the
AUTHOR

Sasha Enid was born and raised in Hartford, CT. There she obtained a Bachelor of Arts degree in English at the University of Saint Joseph in West Hartford. While in Connecticut, Sasha was actively involved with the youth in churches and schools. Since then, Sasha has published two books, "With Purpose on Purpose" and "Queen Bees-Lessons from the Life of Deborah" (both available on Amazon).

Currently Sasha resides in Rhode Island where she works for a non-profit organization that works with children and families. Sasha is also an ordained minister and works with the women's ministry at her church. Currently she is also the Director of Education for Revival International Center in Johnston. She also continues to exercise her spoken word poetry ministry in the state of Rhode Island.

OTHER BOOKS BY SASHA ENID:

(All books are available on amazon.com and in kindle format as well.)

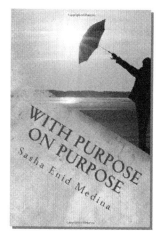

"With Purpose on Purpose" is Sasha's first book released in 2014. It is a book of Christian poetry and reflections. Each chapter tackles a different aspect of the idea that we should live every day intentionally trying to fulfill the purpose for which we were created.

"Queen Bee's" is Sasha's second book, also available in Spanish under the title "Abejas Reinas". This book was released in 2017. Each chapter covers a different lesson that the modern day woman can learn from the life of Deborah who was a prophet in the Bible.

If you'd like to contact Sasha with questions about the book or to invite her to speak at an event, please send an email to the following email address: shewillknot@gmail.com

Made in the USA
Middletown, DE
26 August 2019